Reviews Appearing after CTC was Published

"*Conquer the Crash* woke me up to the realizations of long term changes in the economy and how they affect everyone, regardless of what news or goverments try to do. Before we had read the book, we had some money in savings and a house, car payment, some debt but no real direction of how to use money or avoid the mistakes with money.... Since *Conquer the Crash*, we are now 95% liquid, sold our house at what I believe is the top of the housing market, and are living well below our means with almost 10 times what we started with in savings.... I just wanted to give you my heartfelt thanks BEFORE the crash and your predictions come true (which I believe they will)."

—Kevin McGlothan, email

"I can understand the deflationist warnings of Robert Prechter, the Dean of the Deflationist School. His book, *Conquer the Crash*, is the ultimate reference book on deflation—The Deflationist Bible. The general importance of the inflation-deflation debate lies in its investment implications—inflation means investing in one set of assets, and deflation in a different set of assets. Assets appropriate for an inflationary environment can lose dramatically in a deflationary environment. The opposite is also true—assets appropriate for a deflationary environment can lose value dramatically in a inflationary environment. Whether one believes in a coming deflationary depression or not, one must nevertheless read the book and understand its arguments."

—Krassimir Petrov, PhD (blog)

"Most of what we read about in the financial columns today was brilliantly explained by Robert Prechter in his best seller of 2004 [paperback edition], *Conquer the Crash*....His explanation then of the likely unfolding of events is closer

to what is happening right now than any other commentator present or past."

—Bill Bonner, quoting a reader from Australia, *Bits of News*

"The chapter on real estate was particularly prescient [in explaining] the games played by banks, mortgage brokers and property appraisers—the no-money down loans, the juiced up home valuations, the home equity withdrawals that were bigger than properties were worth—that made the credit binge possible. And there was this warning: Financial institutions that invest in mortgage-backed securities will 'surely regret' it....

"The good news—if you can call it that—is that when the economy, the stock market and real estate finally hit bottom, there's going to be one heck of a buying opportunity. Even Mr. Prechter agrees on that. So it wouldn't hurt to keep some cash on hand, just in case he turns out to be right."

—John Heinzl, *Globe and Mail*

"Prechter is a stock market technician who analyzes historical stock prices and patterns using the Elliott Wave Theory....In 2002 he wrote a book titled *Conquer the Crash: You Can Survive and Prosper in a Deflationary Depression*. In it he correctly forecast a huge credit contraction, brought on by all the mortgage debt issues that we're now facing.

"Reading this book today, it seems as if Prechter had a crystal ball. That's why his current view of the market is so compelling....He says the 'credit implosion' is not finished. Much like Japan, he predicts, we'll have to live through a long period of declining assets, summed up in one word: deflation."

—Terry Savage, *Chicago Sun Times*

"I looked into Robert Prechter's forecasts once I learned that early 2007 is when he positioned his subscribers for a stock market top. I read *Conquer the Crash*, and I have never been so riveted with a non-fiction book in my entire life. He describes

things that had already begun to happen, and he wrote this book in 2002! *Conquer the Crash* describes how we get to, what will happen, and how to survive a deflationary depression."

—David Brown (blog)

"I have to shut my mouth around people who have lost 50% while I have gained 100% in one account. Do yourself a favor and read *Conquer the Crash* without delay."

—Biotechmgr (blog)

"Call him the ultimate contrarian. He is one man who did not flinch in the face of overwhelming majority of market commentators who predicted soaring inflation following the credit-awash policy central banks chose to drown the world in. Instead, he was steadfast in his belief that the outcome would be far more dangerous, i.e. deflation. The script he laid out in his book *Conquer the Crash* in 2002 has vividly played out since August 2007 as the credit implosion finally reared its ugly head."

—*Outlook PROFIT*

"I like the book *Conquer the Crash* by Bob Prechter and have been recommending it to people for years. Rooted in decades of serious research, published in 2002, this book was a frighteningly accurate predictor of the 2008 crash. It explains the 'big picture' of how economic conditions ebb and flow over time, how to profit from them and how to avoid getting caught in the inevitable squeezes that wipe out the unwary (i.e. 99% of the world.)"

—Ken McCarthy, *Independence Day Blueprint*

"Six years from his being a voice in the wilderness on deflation, most has come to pass now. It is frightening, even for the 'prepared.'"

—Tom McGraw, email

"I recently had the good fortune to attend a lecture given by Bob Prechter—his purpose was to update his 2002 book, *Conquer the Crash*....Prechter's brilliant insight is to note that the laws of supply and demand cannot be properly applied to the financial markets because there are no producers to provide the supply curve required for establishing price equilibrium.

"Neither prophets nor intellectual iconoclasts are often honored in their own time....Fortunately, as befits a man focused upon the future, Prechter has responded to this challenge by laying a solid, methodological foundation which can readily be built upon by others interested in following in his footsteps."

—Vox Day, *WorldNetDaily*

"Robert Prechter of Elliott Wave International and the leading proponent of socionomics (social mood determines events, rather than the other way around) has been, in my mind, one of the only analysts/pundits/economists out there who has legitimately called both the deflationary credit crisis and the ensuing rally that we are in now. His unique method tracks the stock market as a barometer of social mood which patterns itself in distinct formations representing fear and greed. The reason I believe that Prechter has been nailing the tops and bottoms of the last few years is because of his contrary position as to the causal nature of social and economic events."

—Matt Stiles, *Futronomics*

"This book outlines brilliantly and simply the rationale for how and why the bubble developed. Prechter will go down in history as a legend for having predicted the secular bull market and now having provided a lucid description of the economic cataclysm that unfortunately lies ahead. I urge you to read this book and give it to your loved ones, as it provides great tactical advice on how to prepare yourself financially. Reading this book could make the difference between agony and comfort over the next twenty years."

—David Tice, Prudent Bear Fund

2018: Last Chance to
CONQUER the CRASH
You Can Survive and Prosper in the Deflationary Depression

Robert R. Prechter

New Classics Library

2018: Last Chance to
Conquer the Crash
You Can Survive and Prosper in the Deflationary Depression

2018 Edition published by New Classics Library

Printed in the United States of America

For information, address the publishers:
New Classics Library
Post Office Box 1618
Gainesville, Georgia 30503 USA
Phone: 800-336-1618, 770-536-0309
Fax: 770-536-2514
E-mail address for products: customercare@elliottwave.com
E-mail address for comments: feedback@elliottwave.com
Web site: www.elliottwave.com

New Classics Library is the book publishing division of
Elliott Wave International, Inc.

ISBN: 978-1-61604-100-7
Library of Congress Control Number: 2018903681

Dedication

This book is dedicated to all my friends and colleagues at Elliott Wave International, who put up with months of my single-mindedness in producing this book.

Acknowledgments

In putting together this volume, I had invaluable help from Robert Prechter Sr., Lou Crandall, Pete Kendall and Jean-Pierre Louvet, who provided expert information that enhanced certain chapters in this book. Rachel Webb, Sally Webb and Angela Hall did the charts and formatting, and Robin Machcinski and Darrell King designed the jacket.

Contents

Preface to the 2018 Edition

In 1982 and 1983, when the majority of investors were afraid of stocks and hiding in money-market funds, the Elliott wave position of the market gave us a unique and valuable perspective. *Elliott Wave Principle*, published in November 1978 when the Dow was at 790, predicted a bull market akin to that of the Roaring 'Twenties. In April 1983, *The Elliott Wave Theorist* made this prediction about the stock market: "In wave V, investor mass psychology should reach manic proportion, with elements of 1929, 1968 and 1973 all operating together and, in the end, to an even greater extreme." As radical as that statement was, I didn't anticipate that the market would surpass those extremes multiple times. Over the past 20 years, we have seen not just one stock market top combining the craziest peaks of the 20th century but *one after another*, in 2000, 2007 and now. Never before have there been three consecutive stock manias of such intensity in so short a time. Within that span there have also been sister manias for real estate, commodities, precious metals, bonds and even cryptocoins, every one constituting a multi-century rarity in its own right. The extent of this manic behavior went far beyond the radically bullish description we issued 39 years ago. Despite what amounted to foreknowledge about an approaching era of nearly unprecedented optimism, I underestimated the extent of every mania that followed. As detailed in recent issues of *The Elliott Wave Theorist*, the optimism toward the stock market of late 2017 is unprecedented by numerous measures.

Throughout this time, my colleagues and I have understood that each market was simply enjoying its turn in the rotation, expressing a multi-century extreme in positive social mood and therefore in financial optimism. One thing that has been crystal clear to us is that payback for succumbing to the enticing lure of these investment sirens would be vicious. Investors who believed in endless real estate gains, the "Peak Oil" scenario, "$200 silver" or "bitcoin at $1 million" paid the price. Today they gorge on index funds and cov-lite junk bonds with the same degree of enthusiasm.

We patiently look forward to the time when Elliott waves, sentiment readings, valuation and momentum indicators finally depict a major bottom in anything. But that time remains in the future. Not a single investment market—be it stocks, bonds, real estate, commodities or precious metals—stands anywhere near a major bottom today. Every one of them continues to show characteristics of being on the left or right side of a historic peak in optimism so extreme as to occur on average only once in decades, if not centuries.

The first edition of *Conquer the Crash* came out in Q2 2002. The stock market had rallied hard from September 2001 to an interim peak for the Dow in March 2002 and for the Value Line Composite index in April. Optimism at that time was through the roof, and I raced to get out the book while that condition was in place. I finished it in March and sent it off to the publisher. You can study a chart of stock indexes and two sentiment indicators for that period in Chapter 31 of *Pioneering Studies in Socionomics*. As it happens, Americans have never been as satisfied with their country as they were then. Figure A plots data from the Gallup polling company showing that CTC was completed at the terminal point of the period of extreme optimism among U.S. citizens that held from Q2 1999 through Q1 2002, a three-year period capturing all the peak readings for the entire data history going back nearly 40 years. From that time until 2008 saw a deep

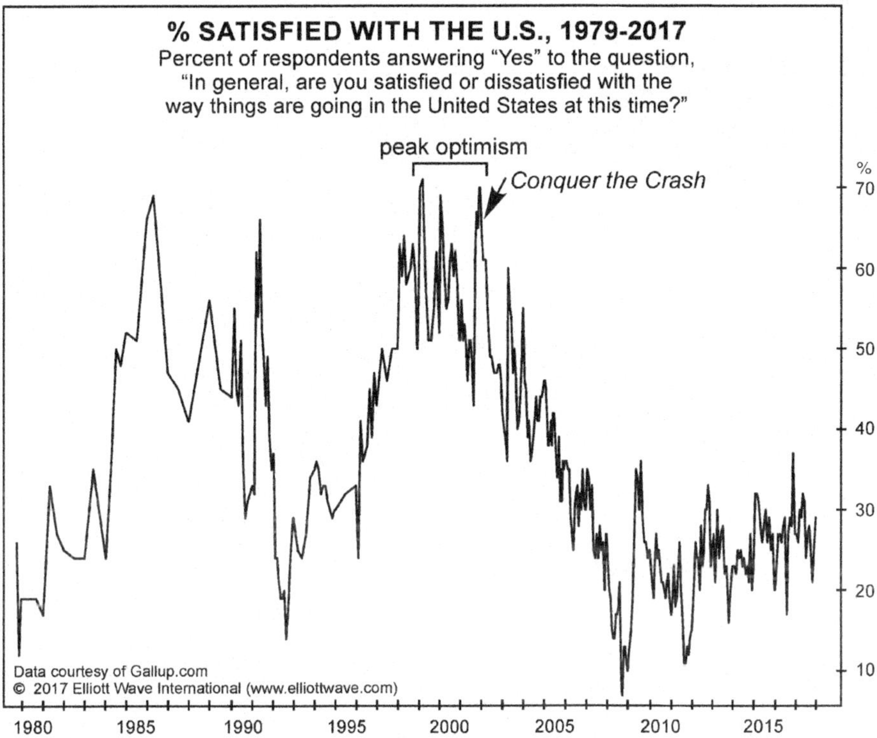

Figure A

decline in the public's feelings of satisfaction. Since then, it has recovered but to nowhere near peak levels. Nevertheless, stock prices and debt levels have soared to record highs, and that's why I'm issuing this new edition.

Record inflating has fooled investors into thinking that stock values are at new all-time highs. But stocks haven't come close to making a new high in terms of how much real money they can buy. Unbeknownst to most observers, the stock market began crashing in real-money terms in 1999. That's when the purchasing power of stocks, as measured in real money (gold), began a plunge that took values down by 86%, as shown in Figure B. It was a silent crash.

The latest wave of optimism, beginning sometime in 2009-2012 depending upon the measure, is about to end.

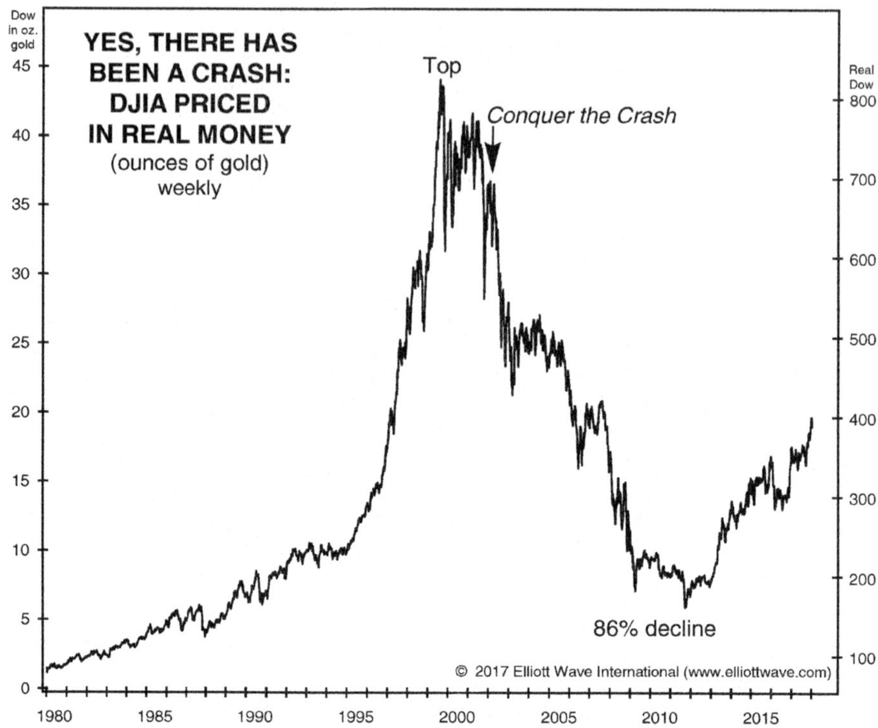

Figure B

Many indicators of investor sentiment show more optimism, and therefore more risk, in the stock market today than at any time in U.S. history — even more than in 1929, 1987, 2000 or 2007. Optimism has also propelled the total amount of dollar-denominated debt to its highest in history and the quality of the debt to the lowest in history. Every financial crash has had the same setup. This one is the biggest yet.

Now it's time for *nominal* prices of stocks to fall, too. That's why I'm issuing this 2018 edition of *Conquer the Crash*, with charts updated through the end of 2017.

You have one last opportunity to exit the stock market at an all-time high. Aggressive speculators should benefit from a once-in-a-century ride on the short side.

EWT's up-to-date analysis replaces the analytical portion of this volume. The sections on deflation, monetary history and what to do have been updated.

Investors who survive and prosper by following the advice in this book will be alone in having ample funds to invest at the final bottom. It should prove to be one of the greatest buying opportunities of all time.

—Robert Prechter, December 2017

Foreword to 2002 Edition

(edited December 2017)

"Look out! Look out! Look out! Look out!"
— Barry, Greenwich and Morton,
via The Shangri-Las

Deflation and depression are exceedingly rare. Sustained deflation hasn't occurred for 85 years. During the past two centuries, there have been just two periods that historians unanimously identify as depressions. The 19th century had one, and the 20th century had one. Amidst today's social psychology, merely addressing the ideas of deflation and depression is considered something akin to heresy or lunacy. Survey after survey shows that most economists believe that depression and deflation, considered together or separately, are utterly impossible now if not *ever*. Most economists believe that the U.S. economy is in a rising trend of perpetual prosperity with moderate inflation, that the Federal Reserve knows how to shepherd the economy, and that if any setbacks do occur along the way, they will be mild and brief. They believe that the Great Recession of 2007-2009 has reset the clock on depressions, so we need not worry about another one for a hundred years.

Despite this overwhelming consensus, I am resolute. This book tells you what the underlying problem is, why the Fed can't stop it, and what to do if you agree with my conclusions.

It may seem to you that the prospect of taking actions that are contrary to the beliefs of a vast array of experts is risky. But a practical point virtually eliminates that risk: If you follow the advice in this book and no financial crisis occurs, you cannot get hurt. In fact, you should profit nicely from most of these suggestions. Even if my outlook proves incorrect, the worst case is that your money will earn less than it otherwise may have. Compare these outcomes to the opposing scenario: If conventional economists, who in the aggregate have a perfect record of failing to predict economic contractions, are wrong again, you will lose everything that you have worked so hard to obtain. You will also blow your chance to make a fortune beginning at the next major bottom.

Here's a bonus: If you end up missing out on some of the investment profits that a decade of prosperity can provide, I hereby truly apologize; I know what it feels like to miss an opportunity, and I will regret that I influenced you to do so. By contrast, if you get destroyed financially by following the bullish advice of economists, money managers, brokers, media experts and the like, they will not apologize. They will claim that the future was unforeseeable and that unexpected "shocks" blindsided them, so *the rock-hard convictions and platitudes that they cavalierly expressed, the ones that you relied upon to plan your financial future*, were wrong through no fault of their own.

There is one catch: I refuse to offer you an excuse to disclaim all responsibility. If you lose your money, your house, your income and your pension in a deflation and depression, at least you can blame the experts for it. You can cry, "I did what they all told me to do!" If you take action after reading this book, I insist that you do so because you agree with my case, not because you are blindly following my conclusions. To be successful in life, or at least to learn something along the way, you have to think for yourself.

—*Robert Prechter*

Part I

An Abbreviated Case for Crash and Depression

Chapter 1:

When Do Depressions Occur?

Depressions are not just an academic matter. In the Great Depression of 1929-1933, many people lost their investments, their homes, their retirement plans, their bank balances, their businesses — in short, their fortunes. Revered financial professionals lost their reputations, and some businessmen and speculators even took their own lives. The next depression will have the same effects. To avoid any such experience, you need to be able to foresee depression. Let's see if such a thing is possible.

Defining Depression

An economic contraction begins with a deficiency of total demand for goods and services in relation to their total production, valued at current prices. When such a deficiency develops, prices for goods and services fall. Falling prices signal producers to cut back production, so production declines.

Economic contractions come in different sizes. Economists specify only two, which they label "recession" and "depression."

Based on how economists have applied these labels in the past, we may conclude that a recession is a moderate decline in total production lasting from a few months to two years. A depression is a decline in total production that is too deep or prolonged to be labeled merely a recession. As you can see, these terms are quantitative yet utterly imprecise. They cannot be made precise, either, despite misguided attempts to do so (more on that below).

For the purposes of this book, all you need to know is that the degree of the economic contraction that I anticipate is too large to be labeled a "recession" such as our economy has experienced thirteen times since 1933. If my outlook is correct, by the time the contraction is over, no economist will hesitate to call it a depression.

Depressions and the Stock Market

Our investigation into the question of forecasting begins with a key observation: Major stock market declines lead directly to depressions. Figure 1-1 displays the entire available history of aggregate English and American stock price records, which go back over 300 years. It shows that depression has accompanied every stock market decline that is deep enough to stand out on this long-term graph. There are four such declines, which occurred from 1720 to 1784, 1835 to 1842, 1852 to 1857 and 1929 to 1932.

To orient you to my way of thinking, I would like to explain Figure 1-1's title. Socionomic theory proposes that waves of social mood motivate social actions. The stock market is modern society's most sensitive meter of social mood. An increasingly optimistic populace buys stocks and increases its productive endeavors. An increasingly pessimistic populace sells stocks and reduces its productive endeavors. Economic trends lag stock market trends because the consequences of economic decisions made at the peaks and nadirs of social mood take some time to play out. The Great Depression, for example, bottomed in February 1933, seven months after the stock market low of July 1932. So, psychological trends create economic trends. This causal relationship between mass psychology and the economy is the opposite of what virtually everyone presumes, so do not be alarmed if you find it counter-intuitive. For a full explanation, read *The Socionomic Theory of Finance* (2017).

If you study Figure 1-1, you will see that the largest stock-market collapses appear not after lengthy periods of market

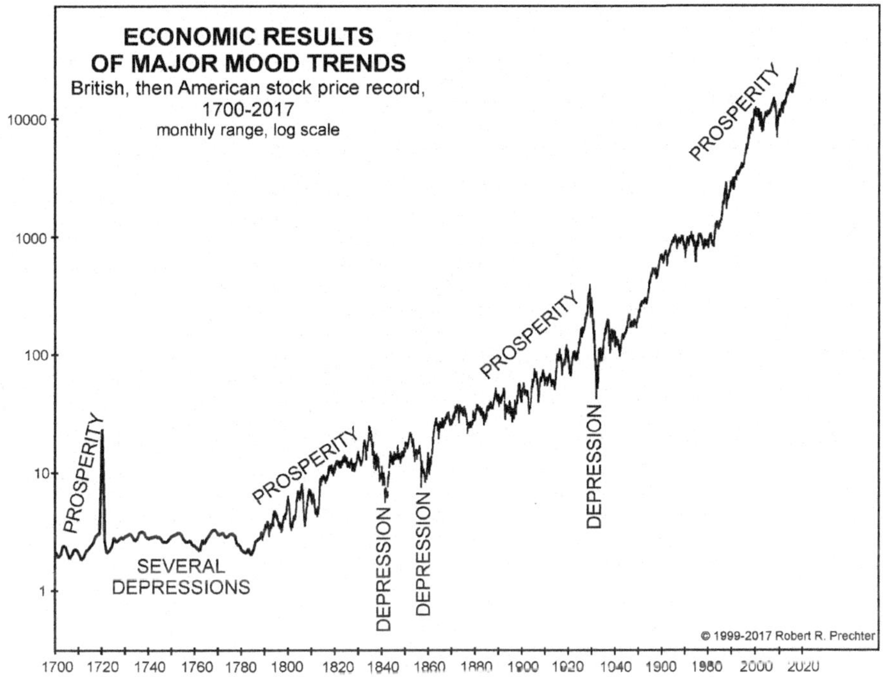

Figure 1-1

deterioration indicating a slow process of long-term change but quite suddenly after long periods of rising stock prices and economic expansion. A depression begins, then, with the seemingly unpredictable reversal of a persistently, indeed often rapidly, rising stock market. The abrupt change from increasing optimism to increasing pessimism initiates the economic contraction.

The graph shows that these reversals do not appear after every period of rising stock prices but only after some of them. How can we tell the difference?

Hierarchy in Finance and Economics

You might be interested to know that almost every smaller stock market decline observable in Figure 1-1 also led to an economic contraction. The severity of each contraction is related to the size of the associated stock market decline.

Unfortunately, this hierarchy in economic trends is difficult to display because conventional quantitative definitions of recession get in the way. Sometimes the economy just fails to breach the arbitrary yet official definition of recession that economists use, so their graphs show no recession when in fact the economy contracts, corporate earnings fall, and economic indicators weaken. In some cases of brief or small stock market declines, the economy simply slows down without actually having a "negative" month or quarter, but an effect occurs nevertheless.

Modern attempts to quantify the term "recession" by absolute size are flawed. It would be as if botanists decided to define "branch" or "twig" by length and width. The result may denote an "official" branch or twig, but the definition would obscure the actual continuum of sizes attending parts of trees. Likewise, attempted quantifications of the term "recession" derive from and foster misunderstanding with respect to the hierarchical nature of economic expansion and contraction. It would be far better for economists to adopt the perspective of the Wave Principle, a model of hierarchically patterned financial market change, as presented in the next chapter.

Chapter 2:

When Do Stock Markets Turn from Up to Down?

We see that depressions accompany major stock market declines. So, if we can predict those rare and dramatic bear markets, we can predict depressions. Can we do that?

The Stock Market Is Patterned

In a series of books and articles published from 1938 to 1946 (available in *R.N. Elliott's Masterworks*, 1994), Ralph Nelson Elliott described the stock market as a fractal. A fractal is an object that is similarly shaped — regularly or irregularly — at different scales.

A classic example of a self-identical fractal is nested squares. One square is surrounded by eight squares of the same size, which forms a larger square, which is surrounded by eight squares of that larger size, and so on.

A classic example of an indefinite self-similar fractal is the line that delineates a seacoast. When viewed from space, a seacoast has certain irregularity of contour. If we were to drop to ten miles above the earth, we would see only a portion of the seacoast, but the irregularity of contour of that portion would resemble that of the whole. From a hundred feet up in a balloon, the same thing would be true. These ideas are elucidated in Benoit Mandelbrot's *The Fractal Geometry of Nature* (1982) and numerous publications since.

Scientists recognize financial markets' price records as fractals, but they presume them to be of the indefinite variety. Elliott undertook a meticulous investigation of financial market behavior and found something different. He described the record of stock market prices as a specifically patterned fractal yet with variances in its quantitative expression. I call this type of fractal — which has properties of both self-identical and indefinite fractals — a "robust fractal." Robust fractals permeate life forms. Trees, for example, are branching robust fractals, as are animals' circulatory, bronchial and nervous systems. The stock market record belongs in the category of life forms since it is a product of human social interaction.

How Is the Stock Market Patterned?

Figure 2-1 shows Elliott's idea of how the stock market is patterned. If you study this depiction, you will see that each component, or "wave," within the overall structure subdivides in a specific way. If the wave is heading in the same direction as the wave of one larger degree, it subdivides into five waves. If the wave is heading in the *opposite* direction as the wave of one larger degree, it subdivides into three waves (or a variation). Each of these waves adheres to specific traits and tendencies of construction, as described in *Elliott Wave Principle* (1978).

Waves subdivide this way down to the smallest observable scale, and the entire process continues to develop larger and larger waves as time progresses. Each wave's degree may be identified numerically by relative size on a sort of social Richter scale, but to keep things simple, this book's occasional references to specific degrees use their traditional names.

Figure 2-2 shows a rising wave in a manner more consistent with Elliott's detailed observations about typical real-world development. Observe, for example, that waves 2 and 4 in each case take a slightly different shape.

Understanding how the stock market progresses at all degrees of trend gives you an invaluable perspective. No longer do you have to sift through the latest economic data as if they were tea leaves. You gain a condensed view of the whole panorama of essential trends in human social mood and activity, as far back as the data can take you.

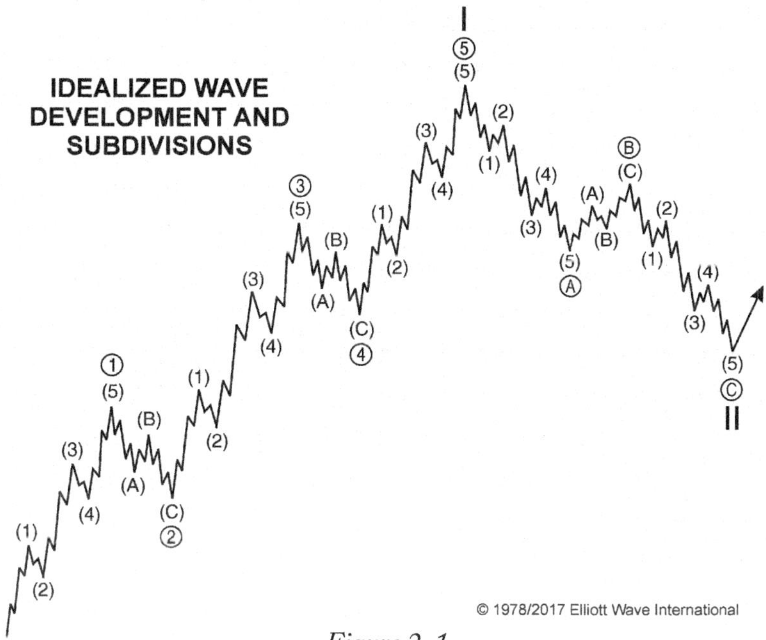

Figure 2-1

Figure 2-2

Why Is the Stock Market Patterned?

For the most part, consumers judge prices for bread and shoes consciously and reasonably according to their needs and means. When human beings value financial assets, however, they must contend with a debilitating lack of knowledge and feelings of uncertainty. They contend with these obstacles to a great degree by forming judgments in sympathy with the opinions and behavior of others. This surrender of responsibility makes them participants in a collective, which is not a reasoning entity. The fact that price changes are patterned proves that changes in the collective's financial valuations are not reasoned, but it also shows that they are not random, either. The remaining option is that they are unconsciously determined. Indeed, shared mood trends and collective behavior appear to derive from a herding impulse governed by the phylogenetically ancient, pre-reasoning portions of the brain. This emotionally charged mental drive developed through evolution to help animals survive, but it is maladaptive to forming successful expectations concerning future financial valuation. The only way for an individual to temper the consequences of the herding impulse and to gain independence from it is to understand that it exists. For evidence of these conclusions, see *The Wave Principle of Human Social Behavior* (1999) and *The Socionomic Theory of Finance* (2016).

Examples of Real-World Waves

Figures 2-3 through 2-6 display advancing waves in various financial markets. As you can see, they all sport five waves up. These five-wave patterns proceeded relentlessly, ignoring news of every imaginable variety, including Prohibition, a crash in Florida land values, Roosevelt's seizure of Americans' gold, Hitler's rise to power and the end of the Vietnam war.

I chose these examples because they display one of Elliott's guidelines, which is that bull market waves often end after reaching the upper parallel line of a trend channel. In many cases,

SAMPLE ELLIOTT WAVES

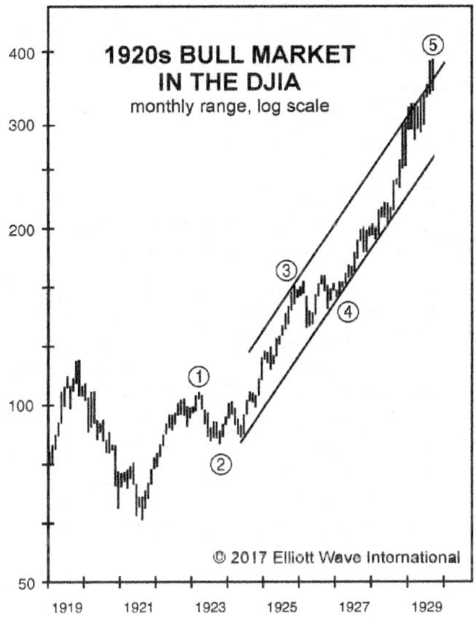

Figure 2-3

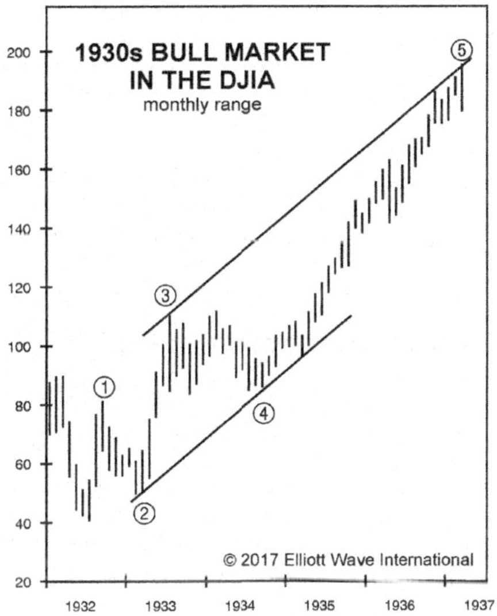

Figure 2-4

Figure 2-5

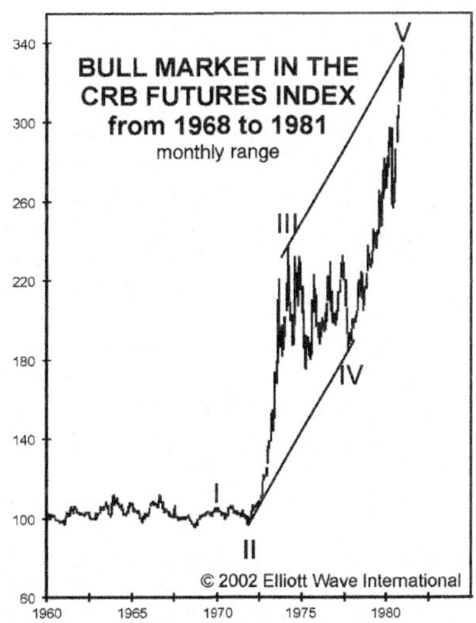

Figure 2-6

the market creates channels in which the lower line touches the bottom of waves 2 and 4, while the upper line touches the top of wave 3 and, later, wave 5.

What Are the Signs of a Topping Stock Market?

Simply stated, a stock market uptrend ends when five waves of a specific construction are complete. The larger the degree of those five waves, the larger will be the ensuing partial retracement of their progress.

Real-world waves are not as tidy as their idealized depictions, just as real trees are not as tidy as any summary depiction of a tree in general. Often third waves are long, with distinct subdivisions. Often fifth waves are brief, and sometimes they go on and on. Using price patterns alone, there can be some doubt as to whether one is accurately identifying a fifth wave or whether it might be part of another wave's extension.

To help overcome difficulty in real-world application, I recorded certain traits that waves seem always to display. Figure 2-7 illustrates some of these traits.

These observations, which I formulated in 1980 after studying myriad fifth waves, tell us four things to look for any time we presume that the stock market is in a major *fifth* wave rather than a first or third wave:

> (1) A fifth wave must have narrower "breadth" than the corresponding third wave, i.e., there must be fewer stocks advancing on the average day in a fifth wave than in the preceding third wave of the same degree.
>
> (2) In a fifth wave, there must be a lesser rate of expansion in the economy and weaker financial conditions than occurred during the corresponding third wave.
>
> (3) Stocks must attain high valuations based on their historic relationship to related data.
>
> (4) There must be evidence of extreme optimism among investors.

These distinctions, helpful though they are, do not eliminate uncertainty in interpretation. Because these wave characteristics are relative, there can always be more development that still

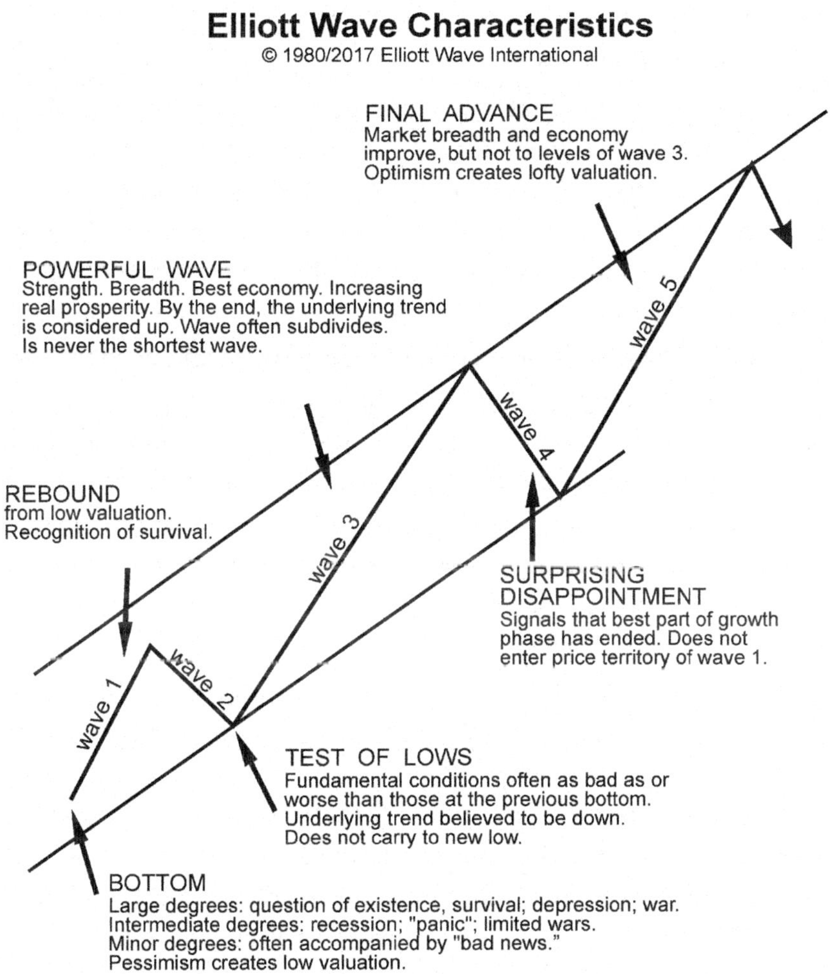

Figure 2-7

reflects these guidelines even after the market has already met the minimum criteria.

Yet we can usually be certain of important things. For example, using the above criteria, we can *know* that a certain wave is — or is not — a fifth wave. The bigger it is, and the longer it has lasted, the more important that information becomes. Early in the process, we can anticipate the ultimate reversal; later in the process, we can begin to assert more emphatically that a downturn is imminent.

The reason that identifying the end of a fifth wave is so important is that when a fifth wave ends, a correspondingly large bear market ensues. That's what happened after each one of the bull markets shown in Figures 2-3 through 2-6.

Recent issues of *The Elliott Wave Theorist* explain why the U.S. stock market is once again at just such a juncture. Among its reasons is a batch of 40 sentiment indicators showing a level of investor optimism and complacency never before achieved. You should review those charts, but sometimes an anecdote can be just as revealing as statistics. The cryptocurrency mania has been crazy, but at least cryptocurrencies have the potential to be a game-changing technology. In contrast, consider this fact about stocks from over three years ago: In 2014, people bought shares of a company that had *one employee*, *no assets*, *no earnings* and *no revenue*, ran a social network with *no members*, was racking up *losses* at the rate of $2 million per year, held $1.6m. in *debt*, promoted its stock through *spamming*, was reported to have insiders linked to *fraud*, registered its website by *proxy* to keep owners' identities secret, and in a filing listed *non-existent headquarters*. That company's stock ran up 36,000% to reach a market cap of *$6 billion* before the SEC halted trading in the stock. (See "Cynk Surges 36,000% on Buzz for Social Network With 0 Members," Bloomberg, July 10, 2014.) A securities lawyer called those buyers "extraordinarily unsophisticated investors." From that state of unsustainably mindless buying, the stock market suffered a setback in 2015-16, but in the two years since then it has gone to a much higher level while attracting even more buyers. What does that remarkable episode from over three years ago suggest about the states of investor optimism and complacency here at the end of 2017, with the Dow nearly 10,000 points higher? Do you think those now gorging on index funds and ETFs are any less naïve? One thing seems likely: These investors will soon learn lessons that will serve to make them more knowledgeable about finance.

Chapter 3:

Implications for the Stock Market and the Economy

If our latest analysis is correct, the U.S. stock market is rounding the cusp of a trend change of Grand Supercycle degree. The DJIA is completing five major waves up that will lead to a three-wave partial retracement of corresponding degree. This means that the decline will not be a moderate setback such as the market has undergone from time to time since 1932. It will be large enough to complete the downside portion of Figure 2-1 if we label its start "1784" and its peak "2017." In other words, the stock market is embarking upon its biggest and longest bear market since that of 1720-1784. If any such bear market occurs, then as we saw in Chapter 1, the economy will experience a depression.

Studies of Manias Bear Out This Downside Potential

In 1997 — when the topic was obscure — I undertook a study of financial manias. Manias are episodes of financial speculation that involve substantial infusions of credit, wide public participation and unprecedented levels of valuation.

A pertinent observation with respect to our current concern is that a mania is always followed by a collapse so severe that it brings values to *below* where they were when the mania began. The apparent reason for this outcome is that so many ordinary people entrust their fortunes to the mania that its reversal brings widespread financial distress, which forces an immense liquidation of financial assets, which in turn stresses businesses and consumers, thereby reducing economic activity.

Figures 3-1 through 3-4 show records of four manias. The ultimate outcome in each case was that values fell below what they were at the mania's start.

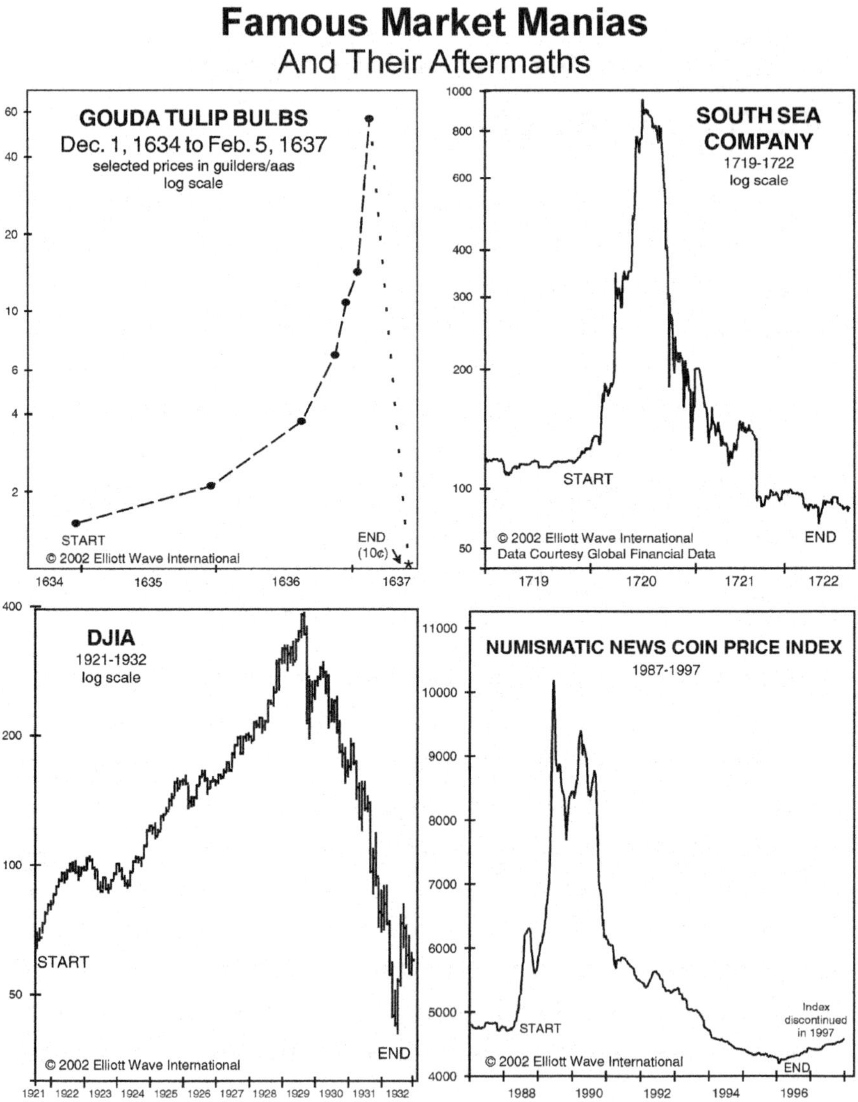

Figure 3-1 through 3-4

A Once-in-a-Century Deflationary Setup

In the summer of 1929, stocks were rising to a new all-time high, bonds had peaked a year earlier, real estate had peaked four years earlier, and commodities were trading at lower prices after having topped out several years before. The setup today is nearly identical. The trends are bigger and have lasted longer this time around, but the progression of events is nearly the same.

The outcome of today's progression should be the same as that in 1929-1933. The primary difference is that the waves culminating today are of larger degree under the Elliott wave model, so the percentage crashes will be bigger.

Implications for the Economy

If the stock market is going to fall far enough to retrace a substantial portion of the uptrend from 1784 and to retrace the price advance during the mania phase, then it will fall far enough to cause a significant contraction in the economy. How deep will the contraction ultimately become?

The proper models for the approaching economic experience are those that accompanied the stock market setbacks of 1720-1722 in England, 1835-1842 and 1929-1932 in the United States and from 1990 forward in Japan. In all those cases, the contraction was an all-out depression.

Part II

The Case for Deflation

Chapter 4:

When Does Deflation Occur?

Defining Inflation and Deflation

Webster's says, "Inflation is an increase in the volume of money and credit relative to available goods," and "Deflation is a contraction in the volume of money and credit relative to available goods." This is just a reverse-engineered formulation whose intended meaning is rising prices vs. falling prices. I do not think this definition is very useful. An economy could have ballooning debt and rising output, and economists would say there is no inflation. Or credit could be contracting while production facilities are being shut down, and they would say there is no deflation.

The terms inflation and deflation should refer to things that can be inflated or deflated, namely money and credit. More useful definitions are: Inflation is an increase in the total amount of money and credit, and deflation is a decrease in the total amount of money and credit. With these definitions, one can discuss monetary matters and economic matters separately without having them forced unnecessarily into a single unit.

The following facts will pertain to our discussion:

- Inflation can be due to money expansion, credit expansion or both.
- When gold was money, money inflation was the rate at which new gold was mined. In a paper- and/or electronic-money system, money inflation is the rate at which new currency is printed and/or electronically created.

- Credit can inflate and deflate under either type of monetary system.
- Deflations could be money-based; for example, if bitcoin were our money, it would deflate as coins were lost or destroyed.
- To date, deflations have always been credit-based.
- When credit inflates to extreme levels relative to the supply of money, deflation is likely.
- When a government operates a money-printing press and there is little debt in the system, deflation is impossible and hyperinflation can result.

To understand inflation and deflation, we have to understand the terms money and credit.

Defining Money and Credit

Money is a socially accepted medium of exchange, value storage and final payment. A specified amount of that medium also serves as a unit of account.

According to its two financial definitions, *credit* may be summarized as *a right to access money*. Credit can be held by the owner of the money, in the form of a warehouse receipt for gold bars or a checking account at a bank. Credit can also be *transferred* by the owner or by the owner's custodial institution to a borrower in exchange for a fee or fees — called interest — as specified in a repayment contract called a bond, note, bill or just plain IOU, which is *debt*. In today's economy, most credit is lent, so people often use the terms "credit" and "debt" interchangeably, as money lent by one entity is simultaneously money borrowed by another.

Price Effects of Inflation and Deflation

When the volume of money and credit *rises* relative to the volume of goods available, the relative value of each unit of money falls, making prices for goods generally rise. When the volume of money and credit *falls* relative to the volume of goods available, the relative value of each unit of money rises, making prices of goods generally fall. Though many people find it difficult to do, the proper way to conceive of these changes is that the value of units of *money* are rising and falling, not the values of goods.

The most common misunderstanding about inflation and deflation — echoed even by some renowned economists — is the idea that inflation is rising prices and deflation is falling prices. General price changes, though, are simply *effects*.

The Primary Precondition of Deflation

Deflation requires a precondition: a major societal buildup in the extension of credit and the simultaneous assumption of debt. Austrian economists Ludwig von Mises and Friedrich Hayek warned of the consequences of credit expansion, as have a handful of other economists, who today are mostly ignored. Bank credit and Elliott wave expert Hamilton Bolton, in a February 11, 1957 personal letter to Charles Collins, summarized his observations this way:

> In reading a history of major depressions in the U.S. from 1830 on, I was impressed with the following:
>
> (a) All were set off by a deflation of excess credit. This was the one factor in common.
>
> (b) Sometimes the excess-of-credit situation seemed to last years before the bubble broke.
>
> (c) Some outside event, such as a major failure, brought the thing to a head, but the signs were visible many months, and in some cases years, in advance.
>
> (d) None was ever quite like the last, so that the public was always fooled thereby.
>
> (e) Some panics occurred under great government surpluses of revenue (1837, for instance) and some under great government deficits.

(f) Credit is credit, whether non-self-liquidating or self-liquidating.

(g) Deflation of non-self-liquidating credit usually produces the greater slumps.

Self-liquidating credit is a loan that is paid back, with interest, in a moderately short time, from *production*. Production facilitated by the loan — for a business start-up or expansion, for example — generates the financial return that makes repayment possible. The full transaction adds value to the economy.

Non-self-liquidating credit is a loan that is not tied to production and tends to stay in the system. When financial institutions lend money to consumers for purchases of cars, boats or homes, or for speculations such as purchases of stock certificates or cryptocoins, no production effort is tied to the loan. Interest payments on such loans must come from some other source of income. Contrary to nearly ubiquitous belief, such lending is almost always counter-productive; it adds *costs* to the economy, *not value*. If someone needs a cheap car to get to work, then a loan to buy it adds value to the economy; if someone wants a new SUV to consume, then a loan to buy it does not add value to the economy. Advocates claim that such loans "stimulate production," but they ignore the cost of the required debt service, which burdens production. They also ignore the subtle deterioration in the overall quality of spending choices due to the shift of buying power from people who have demonstrated a superior ability to produce or invest (creditors) to those who have demonstrated primarily a superior ability to consume (debtors).

Near the end of a major expansion, few creditors expect even weak borrowers to default, which is why they lend freely. At the same time, few borrowers expect their fortunes to change, which is why they borrow freely. Deflation involves a substantial amount of *involuntary* debt liquidation because almost no one expects deflation before it starts.

What Triggers the Change to Deflation

A trend of credit expansion has two components: the general *willingness* to lend and borrow and the general *ability* of borrowers to pay interest and principal. These components depend respectively upon (1) the trend of people's confidence, i.e., whether both creditors and debtors *think* that debtors will be able to pay, and (2) the trend of production, which makes it either easier or harder *in actuality* for debtors to pay. So, as long as confidence and production increase, the supply of credit tends to expand. The expansion of credit ends when the desire and the ability to sustain the trend can no longer be maintained. As confidence and production decrease, the supply of credit contracts.

The psychological aspect of deflation and depression cannot be overstated. When the trend of social mood changes from optimism to pessimism, creditors, debtors, investors, producers and consumers all change their primary orientation from *expansion* to *conservation*. As creditors become more conservative, they slow their lending. As debtors and potential debtors become more conservative, they borrow less or not at all. As investors become more conservative, they commit less money to debt investments. As producers become more conservative, they reduce expansion plans. As consumers become more conservative, they save more and spend less. These behaviors reduce the "velocity" of money, i.e., the speed with which it circulates to make purchases, thus putting downside pressure on prices. The psychological change reverses the former trend.

The structural aspect of deflation and depression is also a factor. The ability of the financial system to sustain increasing levels of credit rests upon a vibrant economy. At some point, a rising debt level requires so much energy to sustain — in terms of meeting interest payments, monitoring credit ratings, chasing delinquent borrowers and writing off bad loans — that it slows overall economic performance. A high-debt situation becomes unsustainable when the rate of economic growth falls beneath the prevailing rate of interest on money owed and creditors refuse to underwrite the interest payments with more credit.

When the burden becomes too great for the economy to support and the trend reverses, reductions in lending, borrowing, investing, production and spending cause debtors to earn less money with which to pay off their debts, so defaults rise. Default and fear of default exacerbate the new trend in psychology, which in turn causes creditors to reduce lending further. A downward "spiral" begins, feeding on pessimism just as the previous boom fed on optimism. The resulting cascade of debt liquidation is a deflationary crash. Debts are retired by paying them off, "restructuring" or default. In the first case, no value is lost; in the second, some value; in the third, all value. In desperately trying to raise cash to pay off loans, borrowers bring all kinds of assets to market, including stocks, bonds, commodities and real estate, causing their prices to plummet. The process ends only after the supply of credit falls to a level at which it is collateralized acceptably to the surviving creditors.

Why Deflationary Crashes and Depressions Go Together

A deflationary crash is characterized in part by a persistent, sustained, deep, general decline in people's desire and ability to lend and borrow. A depression is characterized in part by a persistent, sustained, deep, general decline in production. Since a decline in credit reduces new investment in economic activity, deflation supports depression. Since a decline in production reduces debtors' means to repay and service debt, a depression supports deflation. Because both credit and production support prices for financial assets, their prices fall in a deflationary depression. As asset prices fall, people lose wealth, which reduces their ability to offer credit, service debt and support production.

Credit expansion schemes have always ended in bust. The credit expansion scheme fostered by worldwide central banking (see Chapter 6) is the greatest ever. The bust, however long it takes, will be commensurate.

Financial Values Can Disappear

People seem to take for granted that financial values can be created endlessly seemingly out of nowhere and pile up to the moon. Turn the direction around and mention that financial values can disappear into nowhere, and they insist that it is not possible. "The money has to go *somewhere*...It just moves from stocks to bonds to money funds...It never goes away...For every buyer, there is a seller, so the money just changes hands." That is true of the money, just as it was all the way up, but it's not true of the *values*, which *changed* all the way up and can change all the way down.

Asset prices rise not because of "buying" *per se*, because for every buyer, there is a seller. They rise because those transacting simply *agree* that their prices should be higher. All that everyone else — including those who own some of that asset and those who do not — need do is *nothing*. Conversely, for prices of assets to fall, it takes only *one* seller and *one* buyer to agree that the former value of an asset was too high. If no other bids are competing with that buyer's, then the value of the asset falls, *and it falls for everyone who owns it*. If a million other people own it, then their net worth goes down even though they did nothing. Two investors made it happen by transacting, and the rest of the investors and all non-investors made it happen by choosing not to disagree with their price. Financial values can disappear through a decrease in prices for any type of investment asset, including bonds, stocks, commodities, properties and cryptocurrencies.

Anyone who watches the stock or commodity markets closely has seen this phenomenon on a small scale many times. Whenever a market "gaps" up or down on an opening, it simply registers a new value *on the first trade*, which can be conducted by a small portion of market participants. It did not take everyone's action to make it happen, just most people's inaction on the other side. In financial market "explosions" and panics, there are prices at which assets do not trade at all as they go from one trade to the next in great leaps.

A similar dynamic holds in the creation and destruction of credit. Let's suppose that a lender starts with a million dollars and the borrower starts with zero. After the creditor lends his money, the borrower possesses the million dollars, yet the lender feels that he still owns the million dollars that he lent out. If anyone asks the lender what he is worth, he says, "a million dollars," and shows the note to prove it. Because of this conviction, there is, in the minds of the debtor and the creditor combined, two million dollars worth of value where before there was only one. When the lender calls in the debt and the borrower pays it, he gets back his million dollars. If the borrower can't pay it, the value of the note goes to zero. Either way, the presumed extra value disappears. If the original lender sold his note for cash, then someone else loses. In an actively traded bond market, the result of a looming default is like a game of "hot potato": whoever holds it last loses. When the volume of credit is large, investors can perceive vast sums of money and value where in fact there are nothing but repayment promises, which are financial assets dependent upon consensus valuation and the ability of debtors to pay. IOUs can be issued indefinitely, but they have value only as long as, and only to the extent that, people believe the debtors will repay.

The dynamics of value expansion and contraction explain why a bear market can bankrupt millions of people. At the peak of a credit expansion and bull market, assets have been valued upward, and all participants are wealthy. This is true of both the people who sold the assets and the people who hold the assets. The latter group is far larger than the former, because the total supply of money has been relatively stable while the total value of financial assets has ballooned. When the market turns down, the dynamic goes into reverse. Only a very few owners of a collapsing financial asset trade it for money at 90% of peak value. Some others may get out at 80%, 50% or 30% of peak value. In each case, sellers are simply transferring the remaining future losses to someone else. In a bear market, the vast majority does nothing and gets stuck holding assets with low or non-existent valuations. The "million dollars" that a wealthy investor might have thought he had in his bond portfolio or at a stock's peak value can quite rapidly become $500,000, $50,000, $5000 or $50. *The rest of it just disappears.* You see, he never really had a million dollars; all he had was IOUs or stock certificates. The idea that it had a certain *financial value* was in his head and the heads of others who agreed. When the agreement about price changed, so did the value. Poof! Gone in a flash of aggregated neurons. This is exactly what happens to most investment assets in a period of deflation.

A Global Story

The next six chapters present a discussion that will allow you to understand today's money and credit situation and why deflation is due. I have chosen to focus on the history and conditions of the United States, but it's a global story. If you understand one country's currency, banking and credit history, to a significant degree you understand them all. Wherever you live, you will benefit from this knowledge.

Chapter 5:

Government, the Fed, and the Nation's Money

The Government's Disastrous Reign over U.S. Money

Very few people know that the United States did not create a monetary unit pegged to "buy" some amount of metal, as if the dollar were some kind of money independent of metal. In 1792, Congress passed the U.S. Coinage Act, which defined a dollar as a coin containing 371.25 grains of silver and 44.75 grains of alloy. Congress did not say a dollar was *worth* that amount of metal; it *was* that amount of metal. A dollar, then, was a unit of weight, like a gram, ounce or pound. Since the alloy portion of the coin was nearly worthless, a dollar was essentially defined as 371.25 grains — equal to 24.057 grams, or 0.7734 Troy oz. — of pure silver. In a nutshell, a dollar was equal to a bit more than 3/4 of an ounce of silver; or, in reverse, an ounce of silver was equal to $1.293.

The same act declared that a new coin, called an Eagle, would consist of 247.5 grains of gold and 22.5 grains of alloy. It valued this coin by law at ten dollars, meaning 3712.5 grains of silver. In other words, Congress, rather than allowing gold and silver to trade freely against each other, established an "official" value for gold so that 247.5 grains of gold equalled 3712.5 grains of silver. This is an exchange ratio of 15:1. A dollar was 0.7734 ounces of silver, and Congress was declaring that a dollar would buy 0.0515625 ounces of gold, so gold was valued at **$19.39** per ounce.

This attempt at creating an artificial parity drove gold coins out of circulation, because the market had determined that an ounce of gold was in fact worth more than 15 ounces of silver. Still trying to establish a workable parity, Congress in 1834 passed another coinage act, changing the value of a ten-dollar gold piece from 247.5 to 232 grains of gold (plus 26 grains of alloy), thereby tweaking the gold/silver ratio closer to 16:1. Now gold was pegged at 23.2 grains, or 0.04833 ounces, per dollar, so gold was then valued at **$20.69** per ounce.

This adjustment was no remedy, because after gold was discovered in California the market quickly valued silver higher than gold, thus driving *silver* out of circulation. Neither Congress nor, as we will soon see, the Fed, can repeal the laws of economics and succeed at forcing a particular value on anything.

The Mint Act of 1837 tweaked the purity ratio of gold and silver U.S. coins, making it 90%. This change edged the gold content of an Eagle to 232.2 grains, meaning that one dollar would buy 23.22 grains of gold, so gold was then valued at **$20.67** per ounce. A *dollar*, however, was still 0.7734 oz. of pure silver.

The silver standard ended in 1873, when a new Coinage Act scrapped the definition of a dollar as a certain weight of silver and adopted a new standard based on the weight of gold, maintaining the formula of $1 = 1/20.67 ounce of gold. The Gold Standard Act of 1900 declared that gold would remain the only standard for valuing a dollar and confirmed that a dollar was 1/20.67 ounces of gold. This law put U.S. money on a gold standard.

In 1913, Congress passed the Federal Reserve Act. This act gave a special new banking corporation the monopoly power to issue dollar-denominated banknotes backed by bonds issued by the Treasury. In other words, it gave the Fed the power, in a roundabout way, to use government debt as backing to issue dollar credits to benefit the government. The Fed issued its dollar-denominated credits on dollars (gold) it never had, the government would never be obligated to make payments in gold on its Treasury bonds, and the Fed would never be obligated to pay out gold for its notes.

The Fed's machinations diluted the supply of dollar-denominated debt, which naturally led to gold's being worth more per dollar than the dollar-denominated credits. Rather than close its pet bank to right the situation, the government resorted to a self-serving solution to the problem it had caused. In January 1934, Congress passed the Gold Reserve Act, under which the government seized Americans' gold, canceled all business contracts in gold, outlawed citizens' possession of gold and reduced the amount of gold that would define a dollar. President Roosevelt personally dreamed up a new value for the dollar, which he pronounced to be 1/35 of an ounce of gold, thus making the new "price" of gold **$35.00** per ounce. In one stroke, he stole 41% of the value of everyone's dollars in a single moment, to the benefit of the government.

Because the Act prohibited U.S. citizens from trading in gold, this new, lower value of a dollar was thereafter applied only to international transactions. To maintain a domestic monetary standard, Congress simultaneously gave the Treasury the privilege of issuing paper dollar "certificates" redeemable in silver at the rate of $1.29/oz., which was its statutory value as established in 1792. With the silver price still depressed from the Great Depression, this was, for a brief time, a "fair" price. Congress passed the Silver Purchase Act of 1934 to acquire silver to back the certificates.

This scheme didn't last even three decades. With the government's continued borrowing and the Fed's monetization of much of it, smart people began redeeming the government's paper certificates for silver, and the Treasury's silver stocks began to dwindle. In 1960, President Kennedy ordered the Treasury to stop printing silver certificates above $1 in value, the aim being to make it nearly impossible for citizens to gather up enough certificates to make redeeming them worthwhile. In 1961, the government's silver stock plummeted 80% as smart people accelerated their pace of redeeming large-denomination bills. That year, Kennedy issued an Executive Order to halt the redemption of silver certificates and urged Congress to let the Fed take over the nation's currency. In 1963, Congress obliged by passing Public Law 88-36, which revoked the Silver Purchase Act and authorized the Federal Reserve to issue banknotes unbacked by money. The U.S. mint continued to make silver coins through 1964 with what silver it had left. By 1965, the Fed had issued enough Federal Reserve notes to overrun the circulation of silver-backed U.S. Treasury certificates. That year, on July 23, Congress passed the Coinage Act of 1965, which declared that commonly used U.S. coins would henceforth contain no silver. The half-dollar coin was reduced to 40% silver. For three more years, the government paid out silver to the few people who brought in silver certificates for redemption, but it ceased doing so in June 1968, reneging on the promise printed on its certificates. The last year that 40%-silver half-dollar coins were minted for circulation was 1969.

The year 1965, then, is the key year marking the official end of metal-backed money in America. The Fed's notes, and even the government's old money-backed notes, became the currency of the land, unredeemable in anything. The dollar became merely an accounting unit. Americans were forced to use the Fed's accounting units and the Treasury's tokens for transactions or go to jail. In other words, it became illegal to circumvent the government's program of stealing value from citizens' savings accounts through the process of issuing debt and having the Fed turn it into banknotes and checking accounts.

Meanwhile, gold was on its own road to complete de-monetization. In 1944, the U.S. had joined a group of other political price-fixers via the Bretton Woods monetary agreement, which, as noted earlier, allowed foreign governments — but not U.S. citizens — to redeem dollars for gold at the U.S. Treasury at the rate of $35/oz. This agreement gave the U.S. government the economic advantage of issuing the world's "reserve currency."

It took just fifteen years for foreigners to figure out that the government and the Fed's legal counterfeiting factory was persistently reducing the value of Federal Reserve notes, thereby raising the value of gold in relation to them. They began quietly turning in the Fed's dollar-denominated IOUs to the Treasury and demanding gold in payment at the rate of 1/35 of an ounce of gold per dollar. Just as silver had flowed out of the Treasury in the early 1960s, gold began flowing out of the Treasury in the late 1960s, but this time it went overseas. For a dozen years, Congress allowed foreigners (and, according to conspiracy theorists, secretly connected individuals) to raid the U.S. Treasury, leaving Fed-note holders with increasingly devalued currency and foreigners (and perhaps insiders) with most of the government's gold.

In 1968, President Nixon issued an Executive Order reducing the official value of a Fed-owed dollar to 1/38 of an ounce of gold, thereby raising the "price" of gold to **$38.00** per ounce. This feeble attempt to stem the tide lasted only three years.

Finally the government had to admit that its monetary ruse had failed. In 1971, Nixon issued Executive Order 11615, which reneged on the government's obligation to pay out gold to foreign holders of the Fed's IOUs. Speaking on television on August 15, the President explained, "The effect of this action...will be to stabilize the dollar." What it really did was complete the eight-year transition during which the term *dollar* was transformed from indicating a specific amount of money to indicating nothing but an accounting unit, thus profoundly *de*stabilizing it.

In 1972, the official value of a Fed-owed dollar was again lowered by statute, this time to 1/42.22 of an ounce of gold, making the gold "price" **$42.22** per ounce. This price was a fiction at the time and still is, but it remains on the books to this day.

In that same year, central banks announced that they would no longer pretend to equate their accounting units to any statutory amount of money but allow them to trade at whatever the market said they were worth. This announcement set governments and central banks completely free to create and spend new accounting units at their pleasure. The Fed's banknotes were still written against Treasury bonds, but no longer would the Treasury's IOUs be paid in gold, silver or anything else, to anyone.

The United States dollar had *been* approximately a twentieth of an ounce of gold or had been *redeemable* for that amount of gold for *142 years*. Following the government's theft of citizens' gold in 1934, the dollar was again redeemable in the original amount of silver, but it was newly valued at only a thirty-fifth of an ounce of gold. The original dollar, therefore, essentially managed to maintain parity to 0.7734 Troy oz. of silver for *173 years*. Then, from 1963 to 1971, Congress through a series of new laws ceased exercising its Constitutional "power to coin money, and regulate [*make regular*] the value thereof." Instead, it outlawed money and replaced it with an elastic (non-regular) unit of account.

The only reason people use the Fed's money-substitute is that the government prohibits all forms of real and alternative money. It requires that all transactions, including the payment of taxes, be denominated in the Fed's accounting units, which, although no longer dollars, are still called dollars.

Section 19 of the original 1792 Coinage Act made the following declaration: "...if any of the gold or silver coins which shall be struck or coined at the said mint shall be debased or made worse as to the proportion of the fine gold or fine silver therein contained [by act of] any of the officers or persons who shall be employed at the said mint...every such officer or person...shall be deemed guilty of felony, *and shall suffer death*." All members of Congress since 1963 — for passing and then failing to repeal Public Law 88-36 — are *de facto* guilty of having "debased" and "made worse" the dollar, but they have hidden behind technicalities in cleverly crafted laws, which shroud the effect of their acts.

A primary source for this review is http://nesara.org/articles/nine_tenths_pure.htm.

The Era of Money vs. the Era of Unbacked Accounting Units

The change wrought by fake money is far, far worse than you might think. Let's look at the timing of the government's abandonment of money.

For 173 years, as detailed above, the United States was on a *money* standard. Congress shifted the basis of the money standard between silver and gold twice during that period. In the fateful year of 1965, shortly after authorizing the Federal Reserve to issue notes as currency, Congress abandoned money altogether and authorized the Fed to provide the nation's currency and the Treasury to issue tokens in place of money, *all without any standard at all.* Dollars became accounting units anchored to nothing. Officials still call the new unit of account a "dollar" and "money," but they are inaccurate on both counts. Or, one might say, they "re-defined" these terms; but they did so without telling anybody plainly what the change meant.

Although a few nuances attend U.S. monetary history, broadly speaking we may delineate the key periods as follows:

1792-1873: silver money standard
1873-1934: gold money standard
1934-1965: silver money standard
1965-present: Federal Reserve accounting units (no standard).

The year 1965 is not just any old year. It is the year that we have long recognized as the orthodox end of the great bull market in the Dow/gold ratio in Elliott wave terms. Figure 5-1 shows this wave labeling, which we first published in early 2001, and Figure 5-2 brings the wave pattern up to date. Thus, the *true bull market* from the late 1700s until 1965 attended conditions under which the country would prosper, the most important of them being a *money standard.* When the bear market started after 1965,

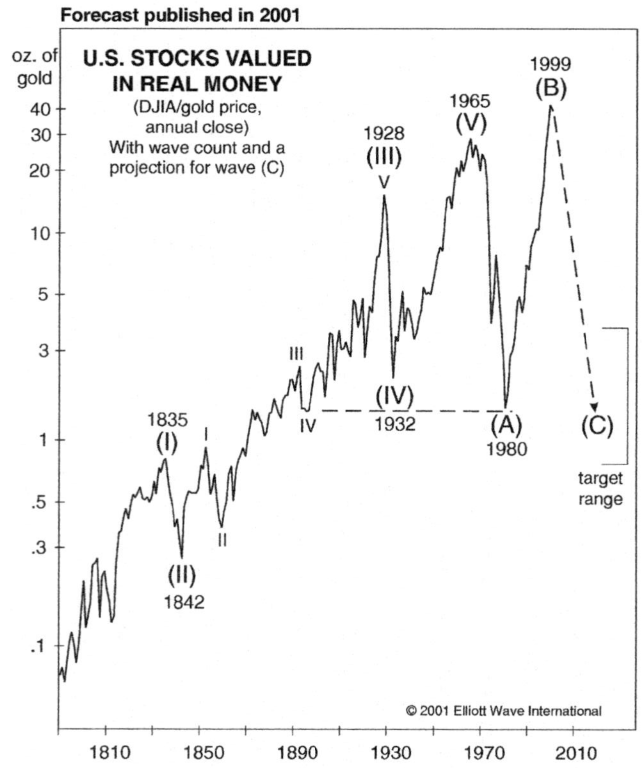

Figure 5-1

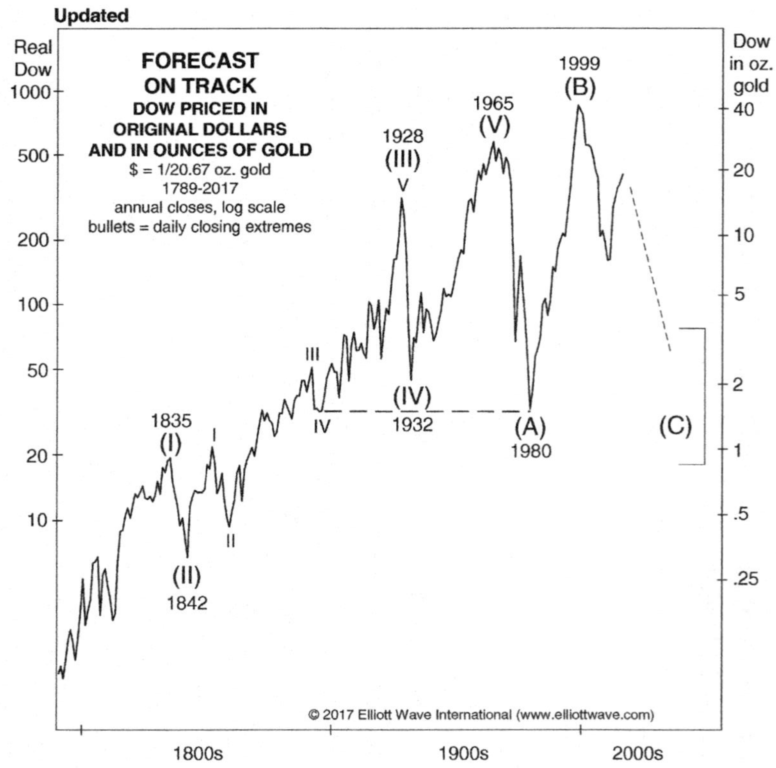

Figure 5-2

conditions shifted to reflect a subtle trend toward the negative psychology of a bear market, one important result of which was the abandonment of a money standard.

(1965 was also year of Medicare, which inaugurated a trend toward deterioration in the quality and affordability of U.S. medical services. Medical services went from almost an entirely free market, with low costs and nearly universal availability, to a market distorted by third-party payers and ossified by hundreds of laws and associated insurance company rules. That trend isn't over, either.)

Figure 5-3 is a chart you have never seen elsewhere. It shows the breathtaking rise in U.S. corporate worth during the bull market period and exposes the stunning net destruction of U.S. corporate worth since the bear market started. The year of the bull market top is when the government shifted the foundation of value for the nation's accounting unit from money to the whims of politicians and central bankers. The difference in result is stunning: From 1792, when a money standard was first made official, to 1965, when Congress abandoned the money standard, the U.S. stock market rose from being worth .09 ounces of gold to being worth 27.59 ounces, a difference of **+30,556%**. Since 1965, when the government abandoned the money standard, to the end of 2017 — despite record highs in nominal terms — the U.S. stock market has had a net *decrease* in value from 27.59 ounces of gold to 18.97 ounces, a difference of -31%.

Had the old trend continued at its preceding average pace, the Dow at the end of 2017 would be up 359% since 1965 instead of down by 31%; and since 1792 it would be up 171,289% instead of only 20,878%. Of course, social mood is in charge of these values, so I do not believe that the Dow *would* be worth that much; it would be worth just what it is today in gold-money terms. But the difference does reveal the power of a bear market to hide its true consequences, including destructive decisions made by the political class.

The only reason people do not know the country's true stock market history and its current real worth is that the massive inflating of accounting-unit dollars has caused a reduction in the value of the accounting unit, which in turn has masked the devastation of U.S. stock values. But Figure 5-3 tells the truth: The bull market ended in 1965; the bear market — which includes a brief run to a new high in 1999 — has been raging ever since; and the accounting-unit monopoly engineered by the government and the Fed has been an intimate factor in the trend toward the financial and economic destruction of what was formerly the most prosperous country on earth.

Despite our delineation of the money era from the Fed-note era, the Fed deserves only part of the institutional blame for the monetary and economic effects of the bear market. Congress is primarily responsible for bloating credit and for burdening the economy, by means of its *debt engines* (FNM, FMAC, GNMA, FFCBFC, FHLBs, student loans), *speculation guarantees* (FDIC, FSLIC, bank and corporate bailouts), *regulations* (OSHA, EPA, EEOC, etc.), *taxes* (income tax, social security tax, inheritance tax, gift tax, capital gains tax, excise tax, gas tax, medical tax, etc.) and *criminalization of enterprise* (via thousands of state and local "licensing" laws and business regulation). But the Fed has helped finance it all. By providing an inflatable accounting unit, the Fed made it easier for the government and its friends to extract purchasing power from dollar-holders, with very few being the wiser. This activity has paralleled the dramatic shift of trend in 1965, from 173 years of mostly rising corporate worth to 52 years of net stagnation and decline, with the worst of it yet to come.

True Stock Values

So, why does everyone seem to think that the country is prosperous? The Dow is closing in on 25,000! The S&P is nearing 2700! But, of course, they're not. In less than a century, government through its debt-creating engines and the Fed through its monetary

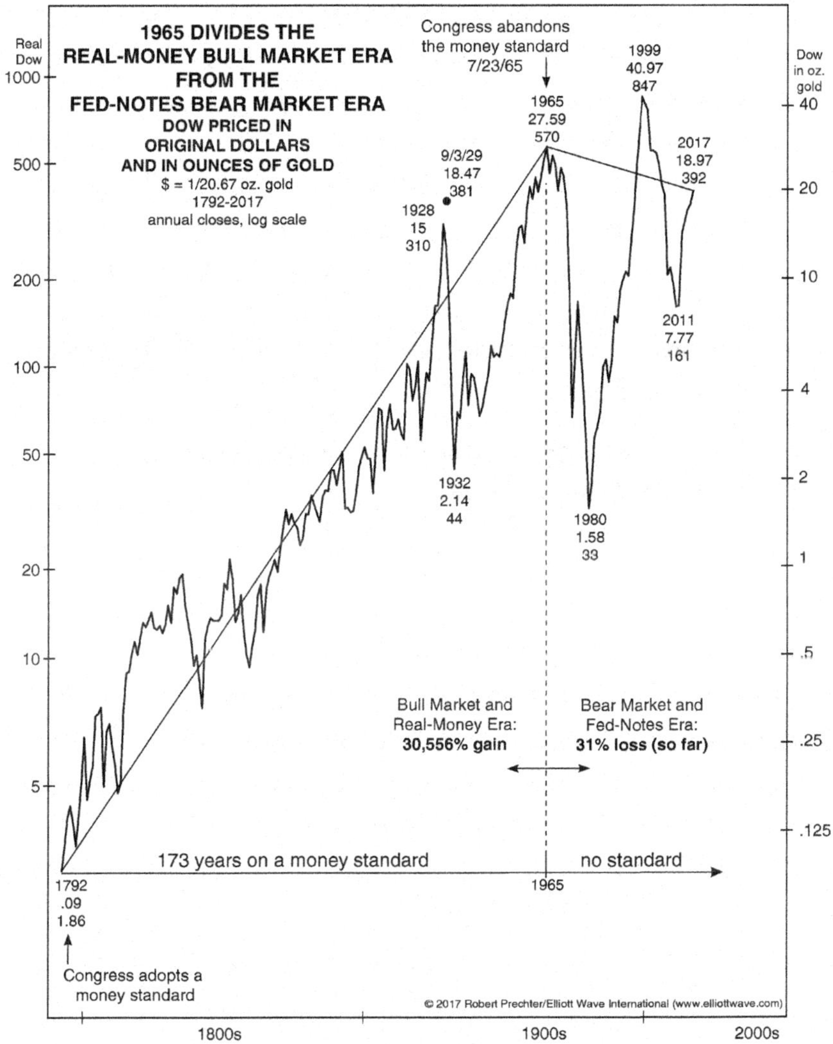

Figure 5-3

policies have managed to reduce the value of the original dollar by almost exactly 99%. From the dollar's original value of **1/19.39** of an ounce of gold in 1792-1834, it slid all the way to **1/1921.5** of an ounce in 2011. With the dollar's recent gain against gold (i.e., gold's fall in dollar price to $1300), the reduction from original value to date is about 98.5%. So, everything today is dollar-priced about 68 times where it would be had the dollar retained its original worth.

As you can see in Figure 5-3, the true price of the Dow at year-end 2017 is not 26,000 but *392*. This is not a made-up figure. This is the Dow's *true price*. That's the price commentators would be citing had the dollar maintained its purchasing power in terms of gold. The Dow at year-end 2017 is worth about what it was in 1929, 88 years ago. The government and the Fed have succeeded in issuing money and facilitating the expansion of credit, thereby obscuring true values and keeping people complacent, even giddy, over their "gains" while they are secretly being robbed.

The Dow's Seemingly Low Real Price Does Not Portend More Gains Ahead

One might look at Figure 5-3 and think that the Dow is cheap in real terms, so it has nowhere to go but up. But thinking so would be to underestimate mightily the destruction that the government has wreaked on the U.S. economy.

Incredibly, the year-end-2017 price of the Dow — 18.97 ounces of gold, or 392 original dollars (normalized to 1837-1933's 1/20.67 oz.) — is ridiculously expensive for what you get: a lousy 2.1% annualized dividend yield, even *lower* than it was at top tick in 1929; a P/E ratio in the high end of the range for the past century and three times what it was at major bear market bottoms of the 20th century; and a 4.99 price-to-book-value ratio (adjusted to the pre-2004 data series) for the S&P, which is two to four times its range from year-ends 1929 through 1987. In other words, the stocks are not cheap; they are historically overpriced. At the same time, stock-market optimism is even more extreme than it was at the Dow's all-time record overvaluation in 2000. The miserable value shown at December 2017 in Figure 5-3, then, comes from a snapshot of the Dow at its second-greatest overvaluation in history and its all-time greatest degree of bullish sentiment. This condition virtually assures that the worst of the devastation of U.S. corporate worth still lies ahead.

Has the Fed Produced Net Benefits?

People speak of the Fed "buying" assets; but it can't buy assets, because it produces nothing of value with which to trade. Congress conferred upon it a monopoly privilege to manufacture new banknotes and swap them for the debts of others (primarily the U.S. government). By this method, the Fed stealthily transfers the stored effort of savers to the issuers of the bonds for which it swaps its new credits, primarily the government. In conjunction with the FDIC, it has benefitted profligate bankers in the short run by enabling them to make profits on dubious loans. It has also bailed out reckless speculators, allowing them to avoid accountability. But in doing so it has sucked value out of all dollar accounts and burdened the American economy.

Has the Fed produced net benefits? No.

Has the Fed contributed to prosperity? No.

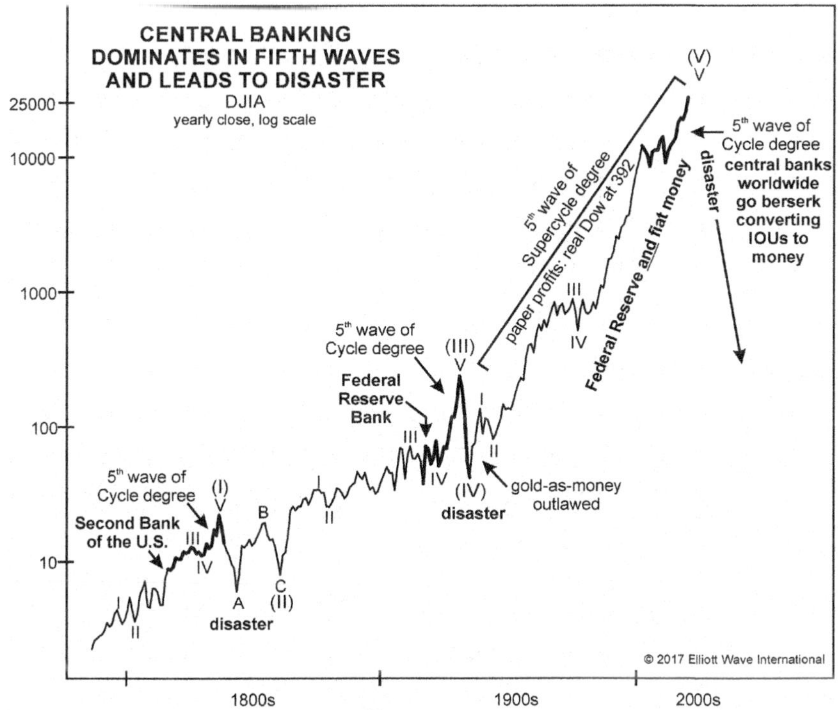

Figure 5-4

On the contrary, periods of central banking lead to disasters. Figure 5-4 shows the history of central banking in the U.S. as it relates to the stock market. The Second Bank of the United States was chartered in time to participate in wave V of (I) in the early 1830s, and the aftermath was two crashes and depressions, ending in 1842 and 1857. The Federal Reserve Bank was chartered in 1913, in time to participate in wave V of (III) in the 1920s, and the aftermath was a crash and the Great Depression, which ended in 1932-3. This time, the government left its monopoly bank in operation, and it has participated in wave (V) from 1932, and especially wave V of (V) since 1982, and even more especially — along with its central bank brethren worldwide — in wave ⑤ of V of (V) since 2009. The huge rise on the chart from 1932 through 2017 is an illusion. As shown in Figure 5-3, the Dow priced in original dollars is sitting not at 26,000 but at 392. The outcome will be no different this time: disaster.

Why the Government Wants All That Money

Figure 5-5 confirms that the era of big government began precisely at the passages of the Federal Reserve Act in 1913 and the Income Tax in 1916. From that time forward, the United States ceased being a peaceful, prosperous country and became a nation of taxation, inflation, debt and foreign wars, activities that reward the political class.

Deflation Ahead

The next big monetary event will not be more inflation but *deflation*, as the huge quantity of accounting-unit indebtedness, built on a foundation of accounting-unit indebtedness, becomes unpayable and contracts.

Debt measures the amount of otherwise-future consumption that has already been consumed. One should not be shocked at the prospect of present consumption collapsing; people already borrowed it all and promised to pay it back. And they will.

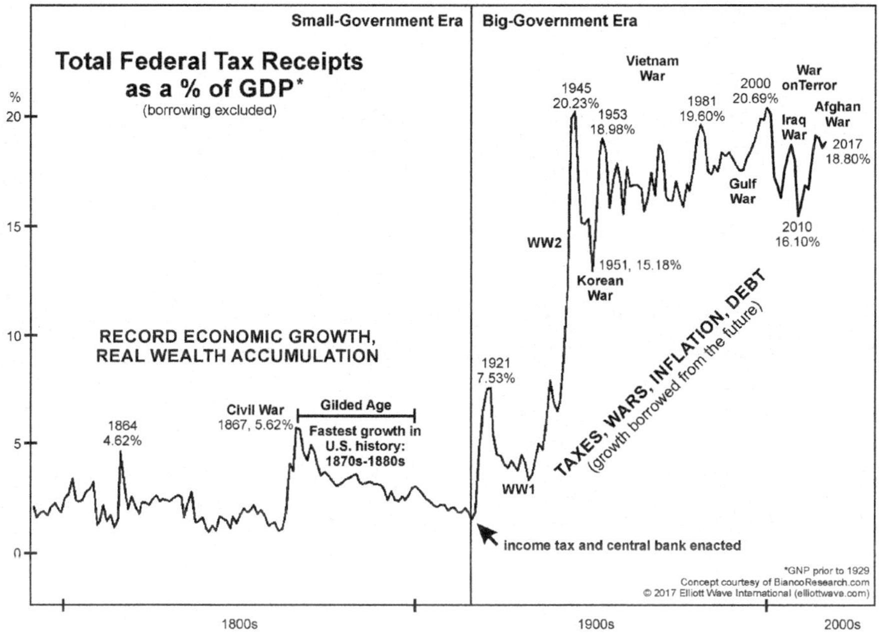

Figure 5-5

After the deflation runs its course, either reform will follow or the government will engage in hyperinflation. But first we have to go through the valley.

Chapter 6:

Money, Credit and the Federal Reserve Banking System

An argument for deflation is not to be offered lightly because, given the nature of today's money, certain aspects of money and credit creation cannot be forecast, only surmised. Before we can discuss these issues, we have to understand how money and credit come into being. This is a difficult chapter, but if you can assimilate what it says, you will have knowledge of the banking system that not one person in 10,000 has.

The Origin of Intangible Money

Originally, money was a *tangible good* freely chosen by society. For millennia, gold or silver provided this function, although sometimes other tangible goods (such as copper, brass and seashells) did. Originally, credit was the right to access that tangible money, whether by an ownership certificate or by borrowing.

Today, all money is *intangible*. It is not, nor does it even represent, a physical good. How it got that way is a long, complicated, disturbing story, which would take a full book to relate properly. It began about 300 years ago, when an English financier conceived the idea of a national central bank. Governments have often outlawed free-market determinations of what constitutes money and imposed their own versions upon society by law, but earlier schemes usually involved coinage. Under central banking, a government forces its citizens to accept its *debt* as the only basis of a legal tender. As noted in Chapter 5, Congress granted the Federal Reserve System this monopoly privilege in the United States in 1913.

What Is a Dollar?

For 173 years, a dollar was defined as a certain amount of silver or gold. Dollar bills and notes were promises to pay lawful money, which was silver or gold. Anyone could present paper dollar bills to a bank or the government and receive silver or gold in exchange, and banks could get silver or gold from the U.S. Treasury for dollar bills.

Today, the Treasury will not give anyone anything tangible in exchange for a dollar bill. Even though Federal Reserve notes are defined as "obligations of the United States," they are not obligations to *do* anything. Although a dollar is labeled a "note," which means a debt contract, it is not a note *for* anything.

Congress claims that the dollar is "legally" 1/42.22 of an ounce of gold. Can you buy gold for $42.22 an ounce? No. This definition is bogus, and everyone knows it. If you bring a dollar to the U.S. Treasury, you will not collect any tangible good, much less 1/42.22 of an ounce of gold. You will be sent home.

Some authorities were quietly amazed that when the government progressively removed the tangible backing for the dollar, the currency continued to function. If you bring a dollar to the marketplace, you can still buy goods with it because the government says (by "fiat") that it is money and because its long history of use has lulled people into accepting it as such. The volume of goods you can buy with it fluctuates according to the total volume of dollars — in both cash and credit — and their holders' level of confidence that those values will remain more or less intact.

Exactly what a dollar is and what *backs* it are difficult questions to answer because no official entity will provide a satisfying answer. It has *no simultaneous actuality and definition*. It may be defined as 1/42.22 of an ounce of gold, but it is not *actually* that.

To the extent that its physical backing, if any, may be officially definable in actuality, no one is talking. Whatever it actually is (if anything) may not be definable.

Let's attempt to explain what gives the dollar objective value. As we will see in the next section, the dollar is "backed" primarily by government bonds, which are promises to pay dollars. So today, *the dollar is a promise backed by a promise to pay an identical promise.* What is the nature of each promise? If the Treasury will not give you anything tangible for your dollar, then the dollar is a promise to pay *nothing*. The Treasury should have no trouble keeping this promise.

People call the dollar "money." By the definition given at the start of Chapter 4, it is. I used that definition and explanation because it makes the discussion comprehensible. But the truth is that since the dollar is backed by *debt*, it is actually a *credit*, not money. It is a credit against what the government owes, denoted in dollars and backed by nothing. So, although we may use the term "money" in referring to dollars, there is no longer any real money in the U.S. financial system; there is nothing but credit and debt, denoted in accounting units.

As you can see, defining the dollar, and therefore the terms money, credit, inflation and deflation, today is a challenge, to say the least. Despite that challenge, we can still use these terms because people's minds have conferred meaning and value upon these ethereal concepts. Understanding this fact, we will now proceed with a discussion of how money and credit expand in today's financial system.

How the Federal Reserve System Manufactures Money

Over the years, the Federal Reserve Bank has transferred purchasing power from all other dollar holders primarily to the U.S. Treasury by a complex series of machinations. The U.S. Treasury borrows money by selling bonds in the open market. The Fed is said to "buy" the Treasury's bonds from banks and other financial institutions, but in actuality, it is allowed by law simply to fabricate a new checking account for the seller in exchange for the bonds. It holds the Treasury's bonds as assets against — as "backing" for — that new money. Now the seller is whole (he was just a middleman), the Fed has the bonds, and the Treasury has the new money. This transactional train is a long route to a simple alchemy (called "monetizing" the debt) in which the Fed turns government bonds into money. The net result is as if the government had simply fabricated its own checking account. The Treasury pays the Fed a portion of the bonds' interest for providing the service surreptitiously. To date, the Fed has monetized $4.5 trillion worth of Treasury obligations. This process expands the supply of *money*.

In 1980, Congress gave the Fed the legal authority to monetize any agency's debt. In other words, it can exchange the bonds of a government, bank or other institution for a newly created checking account denominated in dollars. This priviledge gives the Fed a mechanism —at the expense of all dollar holders — for "bailing out" debt-troubled governments, banks or other institutions, including foreign ones, that can no longer get financing anywhere else. The power to grant or refuse such largesse is unprecedented.

Each new Fed account denominated in dollars is new money, but contrary to common inference, it is not new value. The new account *has* value, but that value comes from a *reduction* in the value of all other outstanding accounts denominated in dollars. That reduction takes place as the favored institution spends the newly credited dollars, driving up the dollar-denominated demand for goods and thus their prices. All other dollar holders still hold the same *number* of dollars, but now there are more dollars in circulation, and each one purchases less in the way of goods and services. The old dollars *lose* value to the extent that the new accounts *gain* value. The net result is a transfer of value to the receiver's accounts from those of all other dollar holders. This fact is not readily obvious, because the *unit of account* throughout the financial system does not change even though its *value* changes.

It is important to understand exactly what the Fed has the power to do in this context: It has a government-granted license to transfer wealth from dollar savers to certain debtors *without the permission of the savers*. The effect on the money supply is exactly the same as if the money had been counterfeited and slipped into circulation.

In the old days, governments would inflate the money supply by diluting their coins with base metal or printing notes directly. Now the same old game is much less obvious. On the other hand, there is also far more to it. This section has described the Fed's *secondary* role. The Fed's main occupation is not creating money but *facilitating the expansion of credit*. This crucial difference will eventually bring us to why deflation is possible.

How the Federal Reserve Has Encouraged the Growth of Credit

Congress authorized the Fed not only to transfer value surreptitiously to the government but also to attempt to "smooth out" the economy by manipulating credit. Politics being what they are, this manipulation has been almost exclusively in the direction of making credit easy to obtain. The Fed makes more credit available to the banking system by monetizing federal debt, that is, by creating money. Under the structure of a "fractional reserve" system, banks were authorized to employ that new money as "reserves" against which they could make new loans. Thus, new money meant new credit.

At one time, banks were restricted by regulation to lending out no more than 90% of their deposits, which meant that banks had to keep 10% of deposits on hand ("in reserve") to cover withdrawals. When the Fed increased a bank's reserves, that bank could lend 90% of *those* new dollars. Those dollars, in turn, would make their way to other banks as new deposits. Those other banks could lend 90% of *those* deposits, and so on. The expansion of reserves and deposits throughout the banking system this way is called the "multiplier effect." This process expanded the supply of *credit* well beyond the supply of money.

Because of competition from money market funds, banks began using fancy financial manipulation to get around reserve requirements. In the early 1990s, the Federal Reserve Board took a controversial step and removed banks' reserve requirements almost entirely. To do so, it first lowered to zero the reserve requirement on all accounts other than checking accounts. Then it let banks pretend that they have almost no checking account balances by allowing them to "sweep" those deposits into various savings accounts and money market funds at the end of each business day. Magically, when monitors check the banks' balances at night, they find the value of checking accounts artificially understated by hundreds of billions of dollars. The net result is that banks today conveniently meet their nominally required reserves with the cash in their vaults that they need to hold for everyday transactions anyway.

By this change in regulation, the Fed essentially removed itself from the businesses of requiring banks to hold reserves and of manipulating the level of those reserves. This move took place during a recession and while S&P earnings per share were undergoing their biggest drop since the 1940s. The temporary cure for that economic contraction was the ultimate in "easy money."

We still have a fractional reserve system on the books, but we do not have one in actuality. Now banks can lend out virtually all of their deposits. In fact, they can lend out *more* than all of their deposits, because banks' parent companies can issue stock, bonds, commercial paper or any financial instrument and lend the proceeds to their subsidiary banks, upon which assets the banks can make new loans. In other words, to a limited degree, banks can arrange to create their own new money for lending purposes. Today, U.S. banks have extended 5% more total credit than they have in total deposits ($12.57 trillion vs. $11.96 trillion). Since all banks do not engage in this practice, others must be quite aggressive at it. Why? Because the Fed stands ready, as "lender of last resort," to bail them out, not with real money of importance to real people — as would be the case in a free market — but with newly created money belonging to no one, whose value is taken from everyone.

Without a reserve requirement, the multiplier effect is no longer restricted to ten times deposits; it is virtually unlimited. Every new dollar deposited can be lent over and over throughout the system: A deposit becomes a loan becomes a deposit becomes a loan, and so on.

Some economists have challenged the idea of the multiplier effect by pointing out that banks cannot create new money, since money lent to (deposited in) banks is money that the lenders (depositors) cannot access. This depiction is indeed the case collectively, but depositors share an illusion that it is not the case for them individually. Virtually every bank depositor believes he has $X in the bank and can get it out anytime he wishes. This is indeed true for an individual on most days, but it cannot be true for many, much less all, depositors at once. To pay out all depositors' money, a bank would have to call in or sell all its loans. Yet if one adds up all banks' deposits, it appears as if there is a lot of money in the system. In fact, deposits are nothing but loans, compounded upon each other. When one thinks of all deposits as money, as each individual does in his own case, there is indeed a multiplier effect: seemingly lots of money where there is little. The real multiplier effect is an expansion of loans, not money. Since the widely shared belief that deposits indicate money is an illusion, a negative trend in confidence can lead to shocking systemic outcomes.

As you can see, central banks have fostered inflation partly by creating money but mostly by facilitating the expansion of credit. This dual growth has been the monetary engine of the historic uptrend of nominal stock prices since 1932. The effective elimination of reserve requirements in the 1980s helped extend that trend to one of historic proportion.

The Net Effect of Monetization

Although the Fed has almost wholly withdrawn from the role of holding book-entry reserves for banks, it has not retired its role of monetizing government-backed bonds. The Fed is legally bound to back its notes (greenback currency), checking accounts and loans with securities, most of which are Treasury-backed bonds. The net result of the Fed's 94 years of money inflating is that the Fed has turned $4.5 trillion worth of U.S. Treasury (and some other) obligations into dollar credits and Federal Reserve notes.

It may surprise you to hear me say that I do not mean to imply that inflation would not have happened without the Fed. Waves of social mood are the primary determinants of credit expansion, and markets are innovative in producing what people want. Base money would not have been inflated to the same extent, but that is a minor portion of the total. If you want to understand how waves of social mood regulate credit, see Chapter 23 of *The Socionomic Theory of Finance*.

So, why all this discussion of central banking? The first problem with the Fed is that it is a government-granted monopoly, serving the interests of the government and its favored beneficiaries — primarily banks but in 2008 also insurance companies — at the expense of savers. The second problem is that its status as lender of last resort, with no statutory limit on its loans, has encouraged bankers to overlend to an extremely dangerous degree. The third problem, which extends from the first two, is that the Fed's powers and mythical status have turned what might have been merely a widespread financial precariousness into a sytemic one.

For Information

There is much information available on the Fed's activities, but nowhere have I found a concise summary such as presented in this chapter. If you would like to learn more, I can start you on your search. For a positive spin on the Fed's value, contact the Fed itself or any conventional economist. For a less rosy view, contact the Foundation for the Advancement of Monetary Education or join the Ludwig von Mises Institute and order a copy of its 150- page paperback, *The Case Against the Fed*, by Murray N. Rothbard, from www.mises.org/catalog.asp. The most knowledgeable source that I have found with respect to the workings of the Federal Reserve System is Lou Crandall of Wrightson Associates, publisher of *The Money Market Observer*, a service for traders. Contact information is as follows:

The Money Market Observer
Wrightson Associates
Chief Economist: Lou Crandall
Website: www.wrightson.com
Email: sales@wrightson.com
Address: Harborside Financial Center, Plaza V
Jersey City, NJ 07311
Phone: 212-815-6540
Fax: 212-341-9253

Federal Reserve
Website: www.federalreserve.gov
Phone: 202-452-3819

Ludwig von Mises Institute
Website: www.mises.org
Email: contact@mises.org
Address: 518 West Magnolia Avenue,
Auburn, AL 36832
Phone: 334-321-2100
Fax: 334-321-2119
Book catalog: www.mises.org/store/Books-C1.aspx

Foundation for the Advancement of Monetary Education
Website: www.fame.org
Email: info@fame.org
Address: Box 625, FDR Station
New York, NY 10150
Phone: (212)818-1206
Fax: (212) 818-1197

Chapter 7:

What Makes Deflation Likely Today?

Following the Great Depression, the Fed and the U.S. government embarked on a program, sometimes consciously and sometimes not, both of increasing the creation of new money and credit and of bolstering the confidence of lenders and borrowers so as to facilitate the expansion of credit. These policies both accommodated and encouraged the expansionary trend of the 'Teens and 1920s, which ended in bust. A far larger expansionary trend began in 1934 and accelerated in 2008.

Other governments and central banks have followed similar policies. The International Monetary Fund and the World Bank, funded mostly by the U.S. taxpayer, have extended immense credit around the globe. Their policies have supported nearly continuous worldwide inflation. As a result, the global financial system is gorged with debt.

Conventional economists excuse and praise this system under the erroneous belief that using force to increase the availability of money and credit promotes economic growth, which is terribly false. It appears to do so for a while, but in the long run, the cost of servicing the swollen mass of debt destroys the economy.

A House of (Credit) Cards

The value of credit that has been extended worldwide is unprecedented. United States entities of all types owe a total of $68.5 trillion dollars.

The biggest problem is that most of this debt is of the non-self-liquidating type. Much of it comprises loans to governments, investment loans for buying stock, real estate and bitcoins, and loans for everyday consumer items and services, none of which has any production tied to it. Even a lot of corporate debt is non-self-liquidating, since so much of corporate activity these days is related to finance rather than production.

This $68.5 trillion figure, moreover, does not include government guarantees such as bank deposit insurance, unfunded Social Security obligations, and so on, which adds another $112.4 trillion or so to that figure, according to USdebtclock.com. It also does not take into account U.S. banks' exposure to an estimated $230 trillion worth of derivatives at representative value (equaling ten full years' worth of U.S. GDP), which could turn into IOUs for more money than their issuers imagine. Then there is the problem of $20 trillion of fixed income payments promised by public and private pension funds, much of which are dangerously underfunded.

Figures 7-1 through 7-4 show some aspects of both the amazing *growth* in debt — as much as 152 fold since 1949 — and the astonishing *extent* of indebtedness today among corporations, governments and the public, both in terms of total dollars' worth and as a percent of GDP.

The total debts incurred by consumers and non-financial — i.e., manufacturing and service — businesses have just reached new all-time highs, as shown in Figures 7-3 and 7-4. This is *not* self-liquidating debt, the kind spent on plant and equipment. Far from it. It is being used to finance LBOs, stock dividends, mergers, acquisitions and stock buybacks. In other words, even non-financial companies have become financially oriented, and they are playing the game by borrowing.

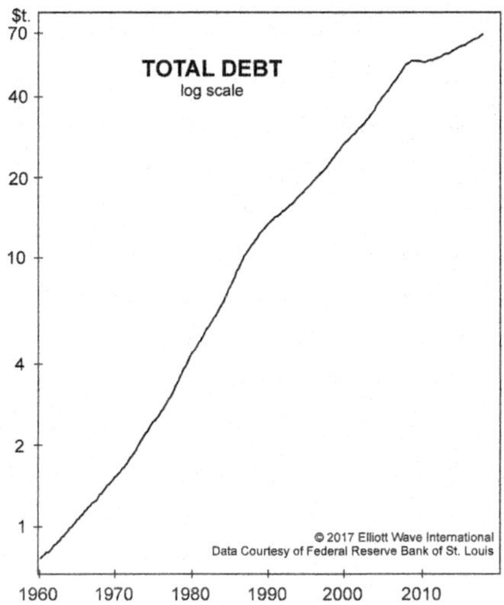

Figure 7-1

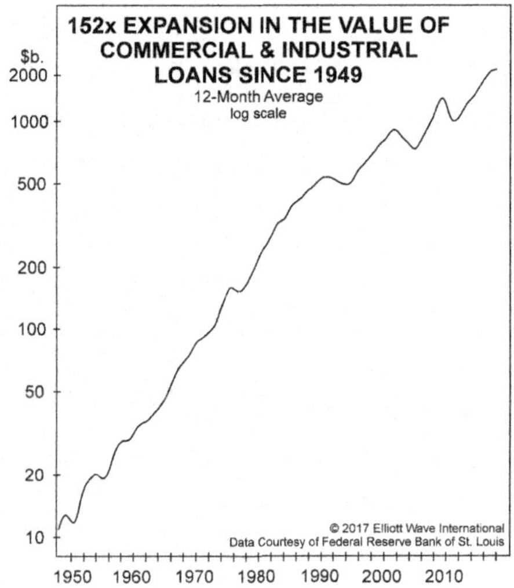

Figure 7-2

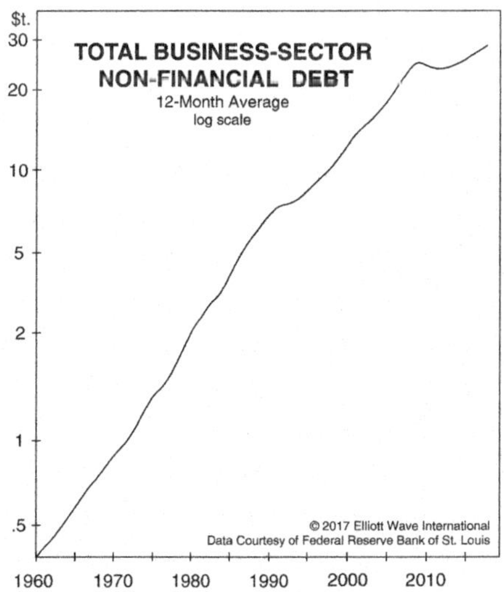

Figure 7-3

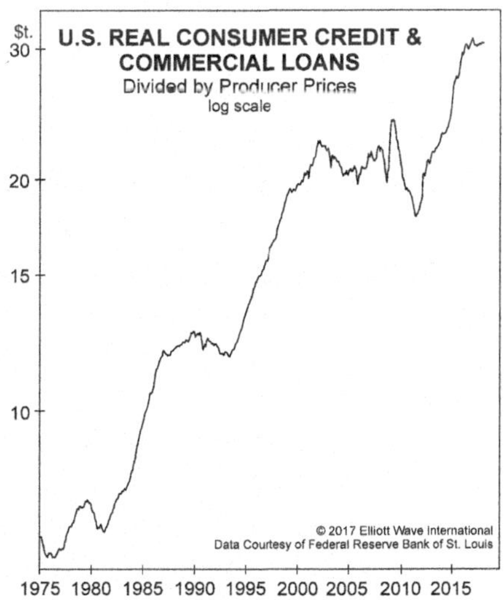

Figure 7-4

Figure 7-5 shows that after a brief contraction in 2008-9, the private debt market has once again been soaring to new highs. Figure 7-6 shows that government increased its indebtedness by a tremendous amount when private debt stalled, and it hasn't stopped doing so yet.

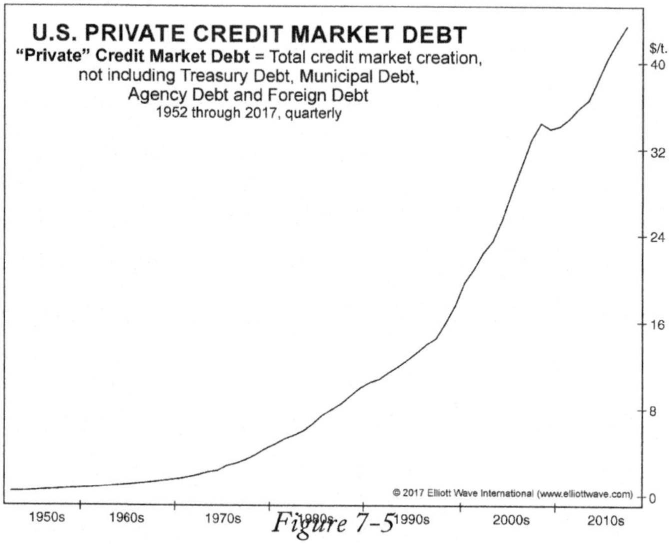

Figure 7-5

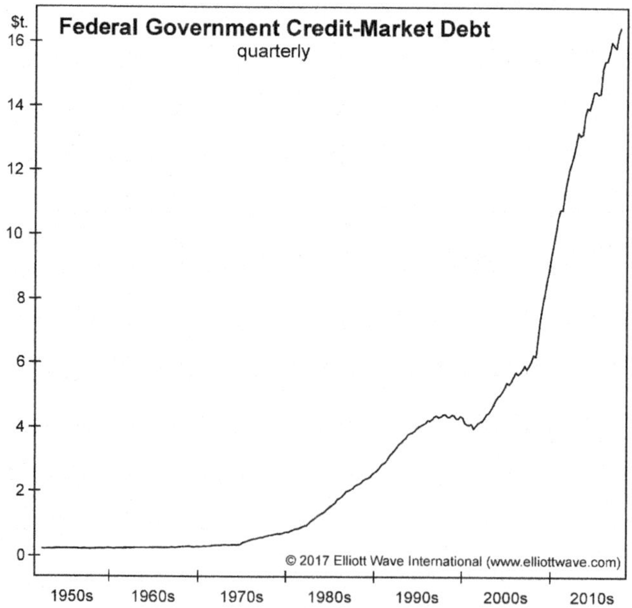

Figure 7-6

One of the things keeping total debt from falling further is the tremendous increase in student loans, as you can see in Figure 7-7. Total student debt has reached $1.49 trillion. Although this is private debt held by individuals, it is promoted and backed by the government, the same conditions that jacked up real estate debt before the last bust.

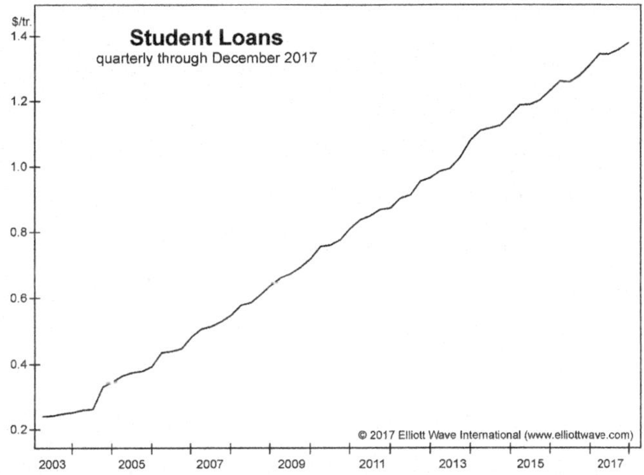

Figure 7-7

If borrowing continues forever, then deflation won't happen. Is student-loan borrowing going to continue its upward trajectory? Not likely. Many students who owe money cannot or will not pay, and the failure rate is rising. Deflation and depression will wipe out most of these debts.

The waxing optimism behind a major fifth wave in stocks supports not only an investment boom but also runaway credit expansion, which in turn fuels the investment boom. Figure 7-8 is a stunning picture of the credit expansion of the 1920s, which ended in a bust, and of that from 1974 to 2017, which is even bigger. The current total debt of $68.5 trillion represents 3.5 times the annual Gross Domestic Product of $19.739 trillion. The ratio is down a bit from its peak in 2009, much as the ratio receded in the late 1920s as the financial boom of that era temporarily juiced the economy, which is the same condition we have today.

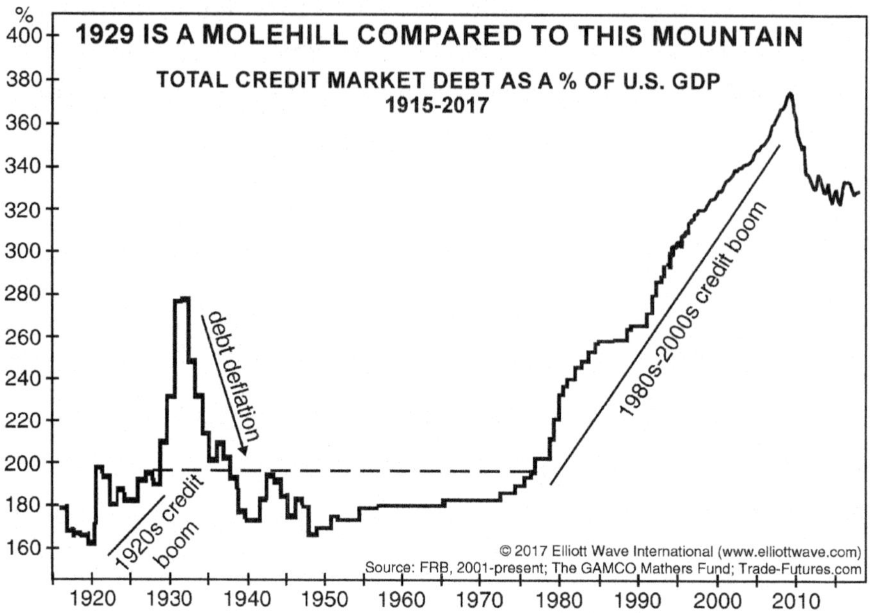

Figure 7-8

I have heard economists understate the debt risk of the United States by focusing on the level of its net debt to foreigners, which is just above $7.8 trillion, as if all other debt we just "owe to ourselves." But every loan involves a creditor and a debtor, who are separate entities. No one owes a debt to himself. Creditors in other countries who have lent trillions to the U.S. and their own fellow citizens have added to the ocean of worldwide debt, not reduced it. So, not only has there been an expansion of credit, but it has been the biggest credit expansion in history by a huge margin. Coextensively, not only is there a threat of deflation, but there is also the threat of the biggest deflation in history by a huge margin.

Stalled Prices for Physical Goods Portend a Deflationary Episode

The main reason investors are expecting runaway inflation is illustrated in Figure 7-9, which shows the value of assets held at the Federal Reserve. The Fed inflated the supply of dollars at

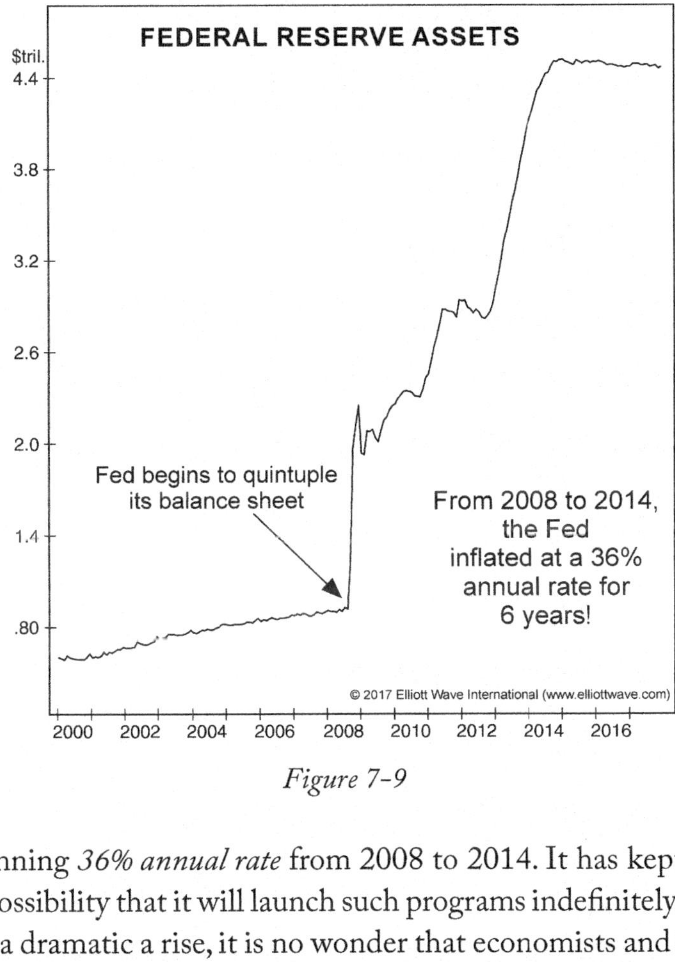

Figure 7-9

a stunning *36% annual rate* from 2008 to 2014. It has kept open the possibility that it will launch such programs indefinitely. With such a dramatic a rise, it is no wonder that economists and investors expect overall inflation to continue.

Given knowledge of the Fed's inflating, many people would expect the Producer and Consumer Price Indexes to have been rising at a rate of 36% annually. But, as you can see in Figure 7-10, the PPI's annual rate of change is stuck near zero and the CPI has been rising at only a 2% rate. Economists have had difficulty explaining why producer and consumer prices have been so sluggish. The short answer is that deflationary psychology is creeping toward gaining the upper hand, no matter what the Fed does.

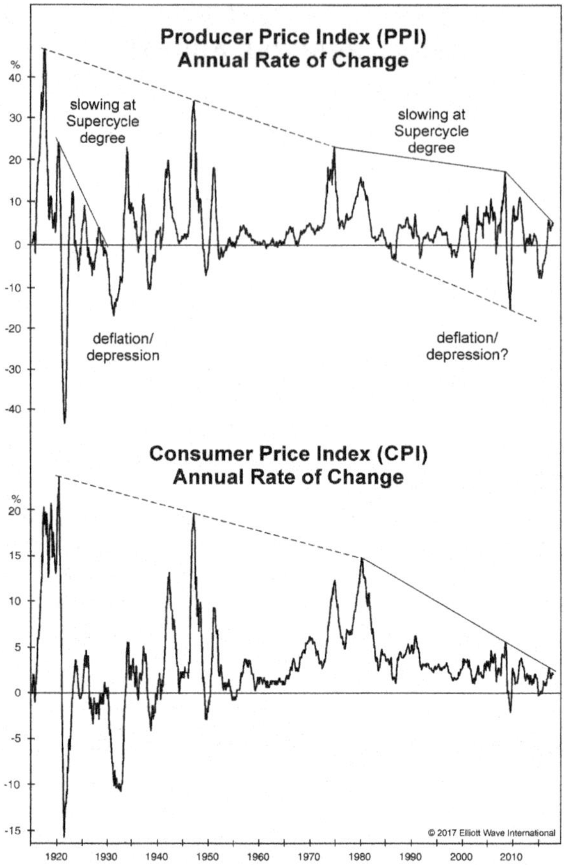

Figure 7-10

Central Bank Lending and Government Borrowing are Failing to Generate Economic Growth

The economy has also been sluggish both despite and because of record inflating by central banks and record spending by governments all over the world. High debt brings economic stagnation and ultimately deflation.

Japan had one of the strongest economies in the entire world, growing at a 9% rate for 20 years up to 1973, and then a pretty strong rate of about 4.5% through 1994. From there, it's averaged about 1% (see Figure 7-11).

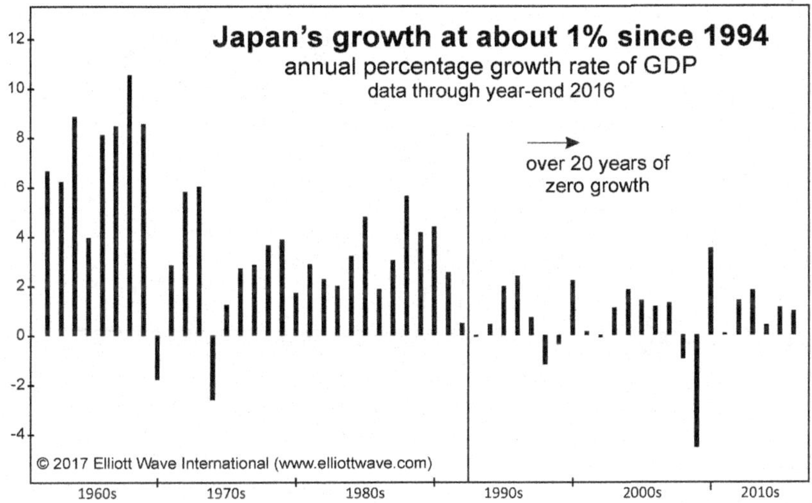

Figure 7-11

The reason Japan is in trouble was expressed in a November 1, 2012 headline from *MarketWatch*: "Japan Is in Worse Than a Deflationary Trap." But it's not worse than a deflationary trap. It's just a deflationary trap. Here's what the article says: "Policy makers have spectacularly failed. Brutal deflation persists. Japanese officials tried monetary stimulus, including zero interest rates and quantitative easing." Does that sound familiar? And here: "Past fiscal stimulus has ballooned the national debt to 200% of GDP." Does that sound familiar, too? And finally, "The most troubling aspect of Japan's malaise may be psychological." That's the key to the whole thing. Psychology changes with social mood from ebullience to conservatism. That's what shifts a trend of expanding credit into a new trend of declining credit and therefore inflation into deflation.

Economic growth in the United States today is weaker than Japan's was in 1989 when its bull market ended. The U.S. economy is dramatically weak relative to the amount of central-bank inflating. Now GDP is hovering around 2.5%, as you can see in Figure 7-12. There is no indication yet of a super strong recovery, despite what economists keep expecting.

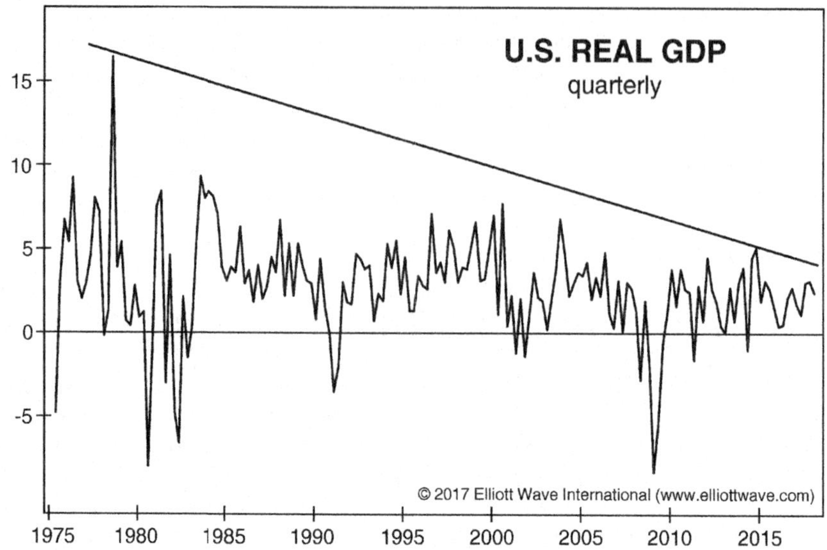

Figure 7-12

Broader Ideas of Money

It is a good thing we have defined deflation as a reduction in the volume of money *and* credit, so we are not forced to distinguish too specifically between the two things in today's world. Exactly what paper and which book entries should be designated as "money" in a fiat-enforced, debt-based, paper currency system with an overwhelming volume of credit is open to debate.

Many people believe that when they hold stock certificates or someone's IOUs (in the form of bills, notes and bonds), they have money. "I have my money in the stock market" or "in high-yield bonds" are common phrases. In truth, they own not money but financial assets, in the form of corporate shares or repayment contracts. As we will see in Chapter 16, even "money in the bank" in the modern system is nothing but a call on the bank's loans, which means that it is an IOU.

Economists have no universally accepted definition of what constitutes "the money supply," just an array of arguments over where to draw the line. The most conservative definition limits money to the value of circulating cash currency and checking accounts. As we have seen, though, even they have an origin in debt. Broader definitions of money include the short-term debt of strong issuers. They earn the description "money equivalents" and are often available in "money market funds," but it's just more debt. Today, there are several accepted definitions of the "money supply," each with its own designation, such as M1, M2 and M3.

The mental quality of modern money extends the limits of what people *think* is money. For example, a futures contract is an IOU for items at a certain price. Is that money? Many companies use stock options as payment for services. Is that money? A vast portion of the population has come to believe the oft-repeated phrase, "Owning shares of a stock fund is just like having money in the bank, only better." They have put their life's savings into stock funds under the assumption that they have the equivalent of a money account *on deposit* there. But is it money? The answer to all these questions is no, but people have come to think of such assets as money. They spend their actual money and take on debt in accordance with that belief. Because the idea of money is so highly psychological today, the line between what is money and what is not has become blurred, at least in people's minds, and that is where it matters when it comes to understanding the psychology of deflation. Today the vast volume of what people consider to be money has ballooned the psychological potential for deflation far beyond even the immense monetary potential for deflation implied in Figures 7-1 through 7-8.

All Debt and No Savings

Figure 7-13 is an important chart, originally published by economist John Hussman, showing the net amount of savings among individuals and the government. It's gone negative because people are spending most of the money they're making and even delving into savings, while government in the meantime is borrowing like crazy. So, this recovery is being financed by entities

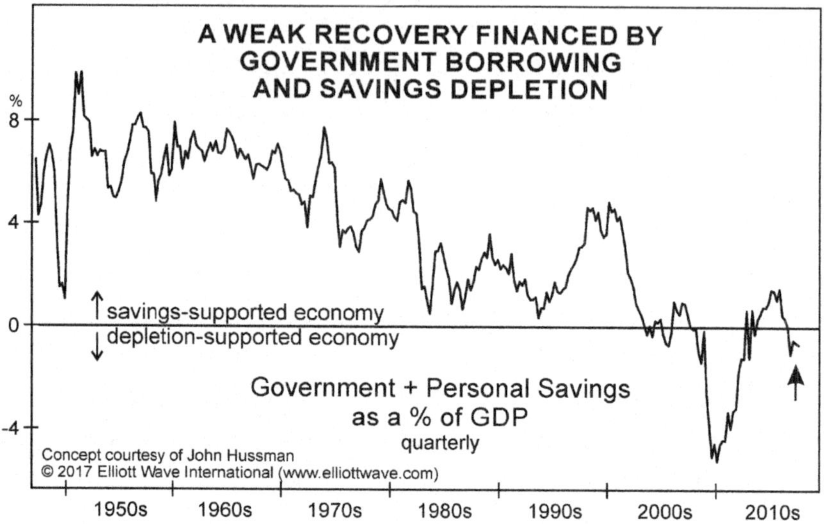

Figure 7-13

using up their savings and borrowing against the future. This trend will not continue for very long. When it reverses, the change is going to be violent.

A Reversal in the Making

No tree grows to the sky. No shared mental state, including confidence, holds forever. The exceptional volume of credit extended throughout the world has been precarious for some time. As Bolton observed, though, such conditions can maintain for years. When the trend toward increasing confidence reverses, the supply of credit, and therefore the supply of money, will shrink, producing deflation.

Recall that two things are required to produce an expansionary trend in credit. The first is expansionary psychology, and the second is the ability to pay interest and principal. After nearly nine decades of a positive trend, *confidence* has probably reached a limit. It also demonstrates a multi-decade deceleration in the U.S. economy that will soon stress debtors' *ability to pay*. These dual influences should serve to usher in a credit contraction.

If borrowers begin paying back enough of their debt relative to the amount of new loans issued, or if borrowers default on enough of their loans, or if the economy cannot support the aggregate cost of interest payments and the promise to return principal, or if enough banks and investors become sufficiently reluctant to lend, as happened in 2008, the "multiplier effect" will go into reverse. Total *credit* will contract, so bank deposits will contract, *all with the same degree of leverage with which they were initially expanded.*

Japan's deflation and its march into depression began in 1990. Europe's started in 2000. China's started in 2007. The U.S. and the rest of the nations that have so far escaped are next in line. When the lines in Figures 7-1 through 7-7 turn down, the game will be up.

How Big a Deflation?

Today, under what is left of bank reserves, there are $2.2 trillion on reserve at the Fed plus $76.6 billion in cash on hand in banks' vaults. This $2.28 trillion of base money backs the entire stock of bank credit issued in the United States. This amount equates to 1/30 of all U.S. debt outstanding, valued today at $68.6 trillion. Those figures do not take into account "IOU-ifs," such as pension promises ($20 trillion), insurance company promises ($6 trillion), Social Security promises and Medicare promises ($112 trillion), of which the base money supply couldn't cover 1/90th in a financial crisis.

Of course, since the dollar itself is just a credit, there is no tangible commodity backing the debt that is outstanding today. Real collateral underlies many loans, but its total value may be as little as a few cents on the dollar, euro or yen of total credit. I say "real" collateral, because although one can borrow against the value of stocks, for example, they are just paper certificates, inflated well beyond the liquidating value of underlying companies' assets. Home and auto loans are backed by collateral, but what will used cars and stagnant homes be worth in a depression? One can also borrow against the value of bonds, which is quite a trick: using debt to finance debt. As a result of widespread loans made on such bases, the discrepancy between the value of total debt outstanding and the value of its real underlying collateral is huge. It is anyone's guess how much of that gap ultimately will have to close to satisfy the credit markets in a deflationary depression. For our purposes, it is enough to say that the gap itself, and therefore the deflationary potential, has never been larger.

Although the United States is a world leader in fiat money and credit creation, a version of the story told in this chapter has happened in every country in the world with a central bank. In China, the debt pyramid, overbuilding, elevated prices for real estate and government support of financial markets are even greater than they are in the United States. All these conditions portend a monumental financial implosion and a corresponding economic depression in China. Europe ranks third for precarious finances, and other countries are not far behind. As a result, we risk overwhelming deflation in every corner of the globe.

Chapter 8:

The Major Downturn in Gold Portends Deflation

Here is excerpted commentary from *The Elliott Wave Financial Forecast* and *The Elliott Wave Theorist* in the month of the high in gold, which peaked on September 5/6 (close/intraday), 2011. Immediately thereafter is an update of our outlook.

The Elliott Wave Financial Forecast, September 2, 2011

Last month EWFF discussed the propensity of central banks to *sell* gold near the end of long price declines and *buy* gold near the end of long price rises. Just last week, Venezuelan strongman Hugo Chavez took the politicization of rising gold prices a step further by nationalizing Venezuela's gold mining industry and moving to repatriate more than 200 tons of gold held in foreign countries, thereby ordering one of the biggest physical-gold transfers in history. A Bloomberg story reveals that central banks are buying with no intention of ever selling, no matter how badly they need the money. "Central banks, net buyers of gold for the first time in a generation, are likely to retain their holdings even if they need to raise cash to counter an escalating debt crisis, according to Morgan Stanley." The story quotes the firm's chief metals' economist explaining why: "Once they've sold, that's it. Buying back would be extremely expensive." Gold experts, naturally, are convinced this cannot happen. Perhaps the strongest sign of a gold top is a recent Gallup poll (below) showing Americans now consider gold to be the best long term investment. Gallup parsed the survey by gender, age, income level and political affiliation and in every single subset, gold won out. It took ten straight years of annual price gains, but now *everyone* is onboard gold's uptrend. It is surely a sign of exhaustion.

Americans' Ratings of the Best Long-Term Investment
Which of the following do you think is the best long-term investment?

GALLUP	Gold	Real estate	Stocks/ Mutual Funds	Savings accounts/CDs	Bonds
Aug. 11-14	34%	19	17	14	10

Gold's wave structure is consistent with a terminating rise. As [Figure 8-1] shows, prices exceeded the upper line of the channel formed by the rally from the 1999 low in what Elliott termed a throw-over (see *Elliott Wave Principle*, p.71). A throw-over occurs at the end of a fifth wave and represents a final burst of buying, as the last sub-waves of a rally conclude. The pattern is confirmed as complete once prices close back beneath the upper line, which currently crosses $1650.

While gold's rise has garnered the financial media's attention, silver's failure to confirm gold's rally goes largely unreported. In our view, this gigantic divergence is critical. Last month we showed silver's five-wave decline from the $49.91 high and subsequent three-wave rally. Silver made one more near-term pop to $44.28 on August 23 to complete wave (2) up. The next significant move should be a resumption of the larger decline that started at the April peak. A decline well into the $20s is a minimum expectation.

—*EWFF, September 2, 2011*

As published on September 2, 2011

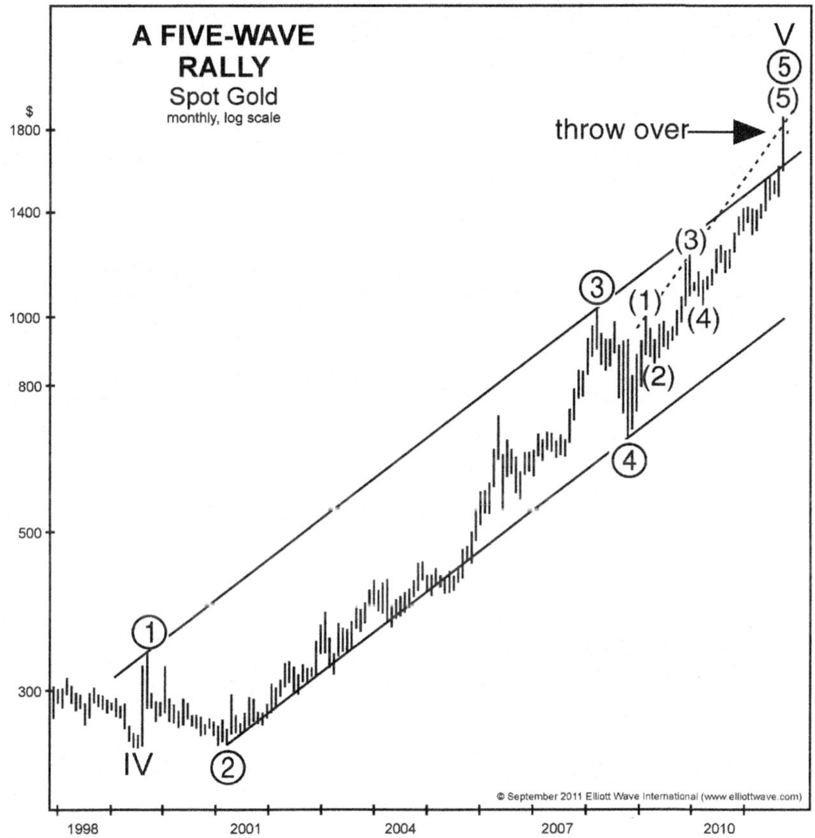

Figure 8-1

The Elliott Wave Theorist, September 16, 2011

The recent reading of 98% bulls among gold futures traders, as reported by trade-futures.com, is not the only indication of the extreme level of bullish consensus on gold. Last November, the president of the World Bank opined that governments should reconsider the role of gold in their monetary systems. Governments thrive on counterfeiting money and hiding that fact. The notion of paying respect to gold, in this context, is a radical idea, indicating how deeply the bullish consensus on gold has influenced people's thinking. Gold's downturn is either already in place or really close.

As published on September 16, 2011

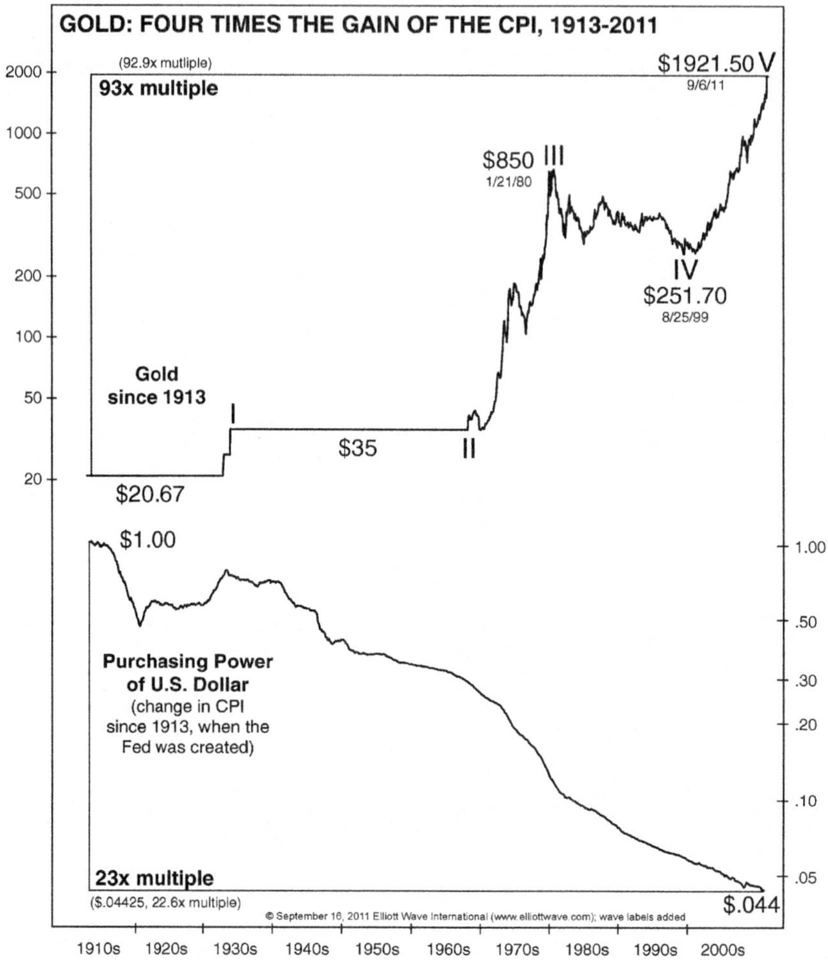

Figure 8-2

Those who argue that gold is still cheap might want to consider [Figure 8-2], which shows that since 1913, when the Fed was created, gold has achieved four times the gain of the Consumer Price Index. To match the gain in the CPI, gold would have to fall below \$500/oz. Granted, the CPI is a manipulated index, so it might understate the true gain in consumer prices. But there is still a notable disparity.

—End of EWT, September 16, 2011

The Elliott Wave Financial Forecast, October 7, 2011

Gold declined 20% in just three weeks in September. But probably the most important feature of the decline from the $1921.50 high basis spot on September 6 is the close beneath the upper line of its long-term channel [see Figure 8-3]. Last month EWFF said such a close would complete a throw-over and announce the end of the five-wave rally from the August 1999 low. Gold's final push was historic, because it ran through multiple sentiment stop signs, as [Figure 8-4] shows. Gold investors assumed these increasingly bearish signals were irrelevant, since prices pushed aside all but the last cluster on their way to September's top. But gold's persistent rise constitutes

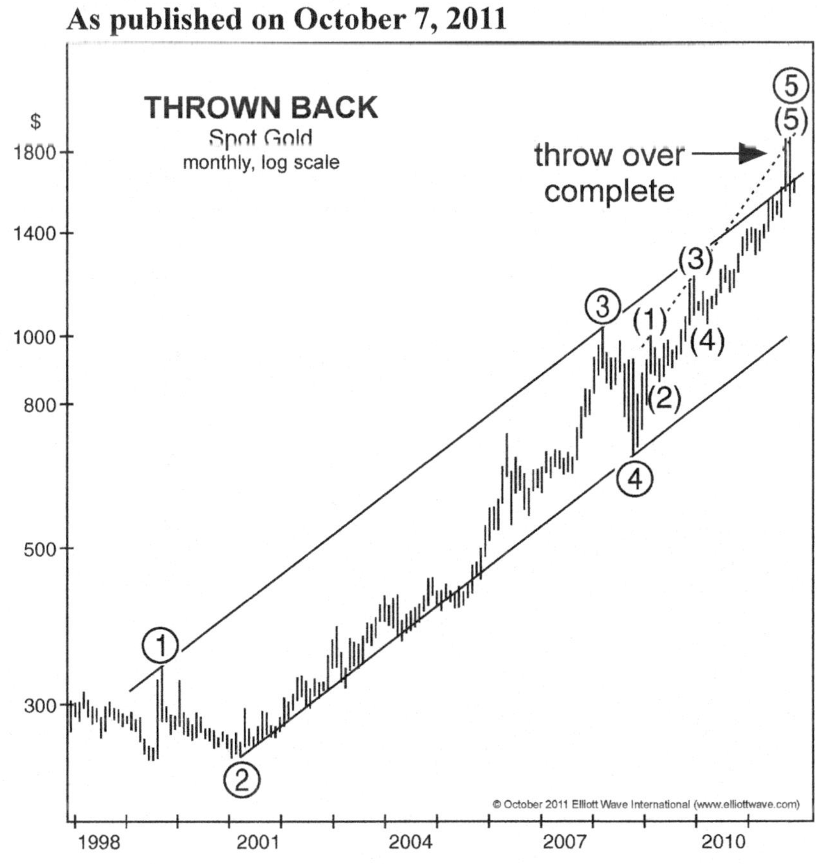

Figure 8-3

a stretched emotional extreme, which will result in an opposite downside extreme, similar to what occurred in stocks after their 2007 peak. The decline that started last month will eventually

As published on October 7, 2011

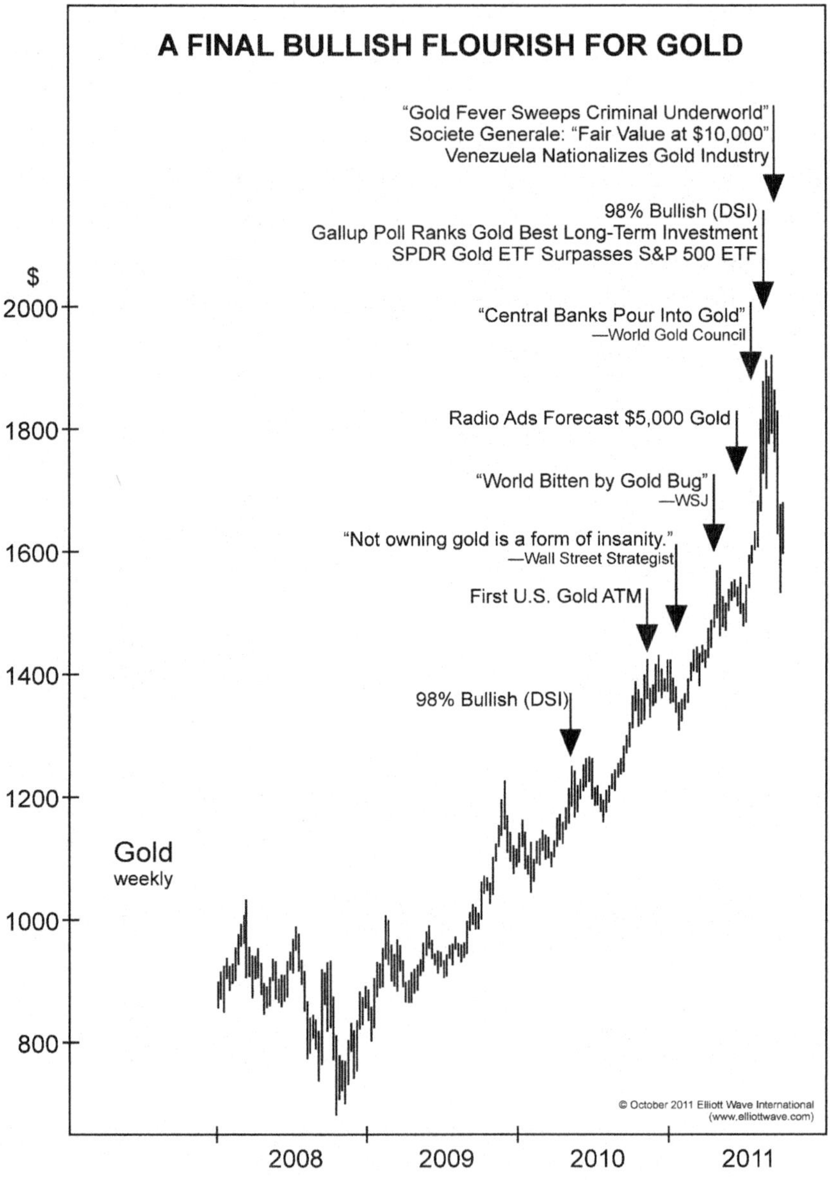

Figure 8-4

correct the entire ten-year long rally, so it should be significant in size and scope.

September also ripped holes in the prevailing belief that silver was a precious metal that would rise as stocks fell. The active futures contract closed the month down 28%, falling in conjunction with stocks and commodities. Prices declined $6.47 on one day alone, September 23, which was silver's second largest daily point decline in modern history. The only decline larger was a $10 drop on January 22, 1980, the day after silver's all-time high. When the precious metals move, they *move*, and the recent decline should carry silver to the next target range in the "low $20s."

—*End of EWFF, October 7, 2011*

Successful market analysis is rooted in irony and paradox. Our gold and silver analysis at the peak in 2011 relied heavily on the converses of five arguments offered everywhere else we looked. Here are two of them, to give you the idea:

1) Central-Bank Buying

An article published on April 19, 2013 quoted a report issued by one of the world's most famous money managers. It reads, "We believe that ongoing central bank purchases and strong gold demand from China and India will help support the gold price in the near term." At Elliott Wave International, we used the very same fact of central bank interest in gold to come to precisely the opposite conclusion on the month of the all-time high in gold.

2) Fed Inflating

In Q3 2008, the Fed began inflating the supply of dollars (the "base money supply") at an unprecedented rate of 36% per year. In 2012, it accelerated its policy by inaugurating a program to monetize government-guaranteed mortgages and Treasury bonds at the rate of a trillion dollars' worth per year, with no time limit. Precious metals bulls seized upon these facts as guarantees that gold and silver would soar to stratospheric heights. This style of argument would be useful if financial markets obeyed the rules of mechanics, but they don't. Here at Elliott Wave International, we again used the very same fact to make the opposite argument. For the full story, see Chapter 2 of *The Socionomic Theory of Finance*.

At the time of the Fed's announcement of QE3, gold was trading at $1770 and silver at $35. The metals edged higher for another three weeks and then began to retreat. At the time of its announcement of QE4, gold was at $1720 and silver at $33.60. Since then, gold has traded below $1100 and silver below $15, each price about 1/10 of what analysts were forecasting.

The last chance to sell (not buy) gold coincided with the Fed's launching of its trillion-dollar-a-year bond and mortgage-buying program. Its program ended in October 2014, and the bear market in precious metals continued for another year. Since 2016, the metals have recovered somewhat and probably have a bit further to rise. But with deflation now on the horizon, precious metals prices should eventually resume their bear market.

Socionomic causality is mystifying to most people. It seems unnatural that a major market rise or decline defy economic explanation. But financial pricing is determined by unconscious herding impulses and regulated by Elliott waves, so mass psychology pushes markets up and down without needing to make economic sense. Nevertheless, we do believe that significant economic changes are in fact afoot, namely a turn to deflation and economic contraction at major degree. When those trends develop, precious metals' weakness will start making sense to observers.

Chapter 9:

Consensus Opinion Concerning Deflation

Seventy-five years of nearly continuous inflation have made most people utterly confident of its permanence. If conventional economists have any monetary fear at all, it is fear of inflation, which is the opposite of deflation.

Another Big Reason Deflation Is Likely: No One Expects It

In 2013, I conducted a test for a presentation to the annual conference of the Market Technicians Association. Here is what I reported:

> You can type just about anything into Google and find it on the web. If you put your query in quotes, Google tells you the number of times that someone somewhere entered onto the Internet the exact phrase you typed in. First I tested "The world is coming to an end." There was a lot of talk in 2012 about the Mayan calendar, so I figured we'd get quite a few postings of this statement. A friend of mine suggested a couple of phrases one would not expect to find, such as "Dinosaurs love to dance." Would anybody ever type that in? Or how about "Plus equals minus," which is a contradiction?
>
> Figure [9-1] shows the results. "The world is coming to an end" got 4.5 million results. A lot of people were talking about the world coming to an end. Believe it or not, 1710 times somebody typed into the Internet, "Dinosaurs love to dance." I didn't read these

Google Search (3/13/13)	
"the world is coming to an end":	**4,510,000** results
"dinosaurs love to dance":	**1,710** results
"plus equals minus":	**48,700** results

Figure 9-1

entries, so I don't know the contexts, but they're there. And "Plus equals minus"— I guess that gives you one reason why the world is in trouble—produced 48,700 results.

I am showing you this list of results so we have benchmarks for comparison.

Now we're going to get to the point. When I typed "Inflation for 2013," there were 47,700 results. On March 13th, when I put this slide together, I also typed in "Deflation for 2013." How many results do you think I got? Remember, there were 48,000 results for "Inflation for 2013," 49,000 results for "Plus equals minus" and 1700 for "Dinosaurs love to dance."

Ready? Here we go.

Take a look at Figure [9-2]. The answer is **5**.

Google Search (3/13/13)	
"Inflation for 2013":	**47,700** results
"Deflation for 2013":	**5** results

Figure 9-2

That's right. Only five times over the entire global Internet did somebody type in "Deflation for 2013." The ratio is nearly 10,000 to 1.

Maybe a quote about deflation is too much to ask. Let's make it easier to get a big number.

First let's type in "Inflation will rise in 2013." This entry produces 50,200 results. On the contrasting side, we will *not* search for a matching quote about deflation. Instead, we will search just on the clause, "Inflation will fall in 2013." Certainly there must be a fair number of people at least talking about the *possibility of a moderation of inflation*, right? Any guesses on that one?

Take a look at Figure [9-3]. The answer is **7**.

Google Search (3/13/13)	
"Inflation will rise in 2013":	**50,200** results
"Inflation will fall in 2013":	**7** results

Figure 9-3

That's right. The ratio is **50,200** to **7**. These results show how one-sidedly the global crowd is thinking.

I conducted one last test. I typed in "The world is coming to an end in 2013." It got 9 results. "Inflation will fall in 2013," remember, got 7 results (see Figure [9-4]). Apparently more people think the world is coming to an end *this year* than that inflation could possibly moderate.

Google Search (3/13/13)	
"The world is coming to an end in 2013":	**9** results
"Inflation will fall in 2013":	**7** results

Figure 9-4

Expecting deflation, to put it mildly, is a contrary opinion.

When I conducted that test, the impossibility of deflation was essentially unanimous. And why not? The Fed was inflating at a record rate, the government had bailed out the biggest debtors, and the stock market was zooming. But since then, despite new highs in U.S. stock averages, the deflation developing in Europe has periodically made news. I re-ran the test today (December 3, 2017) and found some significant changes. The questions posed for Figure 9-1 have about the same results. But the query "Deflation for 2018" brought up 0 results, a significant slide from 5 in 2013. In contrast, there were 37,100 results for "Inflation for 2018, as shown in Figure 9-5." The query "Inflation will fall in 2018" got 5 results, a decrease from 7. That number is $1/2220^{th}$

Google Search (12/3/17)	
"Inflation for 2018":	**37,100** results
"Deflation for 2018":	**0** results

Figure 9-5

of the 11,100 results for "Inflation will rise in 2018" (see Figure 9-6). I am confident that within a few years, there will be a historical "first": more Google results for deflation queries than for inflation queries.

Google Search (12/3/17)	
"Inflation will rise in 2018":	**11,100** results
"Inflation will fall in 2018":	**5** results

Figure 9-6

Professional economists think the potential for deflation is essentially zero. One economist a few years ago told a national newspaper that deflation had a "1 in 10,000" chance of occurring. The Chairman of Carnegie Mellon's business school called the notion of deflation "utter nonsense." The publication of an economic think-tank insisted, "Anyone who asserts that deflation is imminent or already underway ignores the rationale for fiat currency — that is, to facilitate the manipulation of economic activity." A financial writer explained, "Deflation…is totally a function of the Federal Reserve's management of monetary policy. It has nothing to do with the business cycle, productivity, taxes, booms and busts or anything else." Concurring, an adviser wrote in a national magazine, "U.S. deflation would be simple to stop today. The Federal Reserve could just print more money, ending the price slide in its tracks." Yet another sneered, "Get real," and likened anyone concerned about deflation to "small children." On financial television, another analyst (who apparently defines deflation as falling prices) quipped, "Don't worry about deflation. All it does is pad profits." This presumed causality was nowhere to be seen in 1929-33 or 2006-2009. A banker called any episode of falling oil prices "a positive catalyst [that] will put more money in consumers' pockets. It will benefit companies that are powered by energy and oil, and it will benefit the overall economy." This presumed causality was negated in 2008. Others excitedly welcome falling commodity prices as an economic stimulus "equivalent to a massive tax cut," another illusion that 2008 dissolved. A former government economist joked that deflation is "57th on my list of worries, right after the 56th — fear of being eaten by piranhas." On April 29, 2014, Bloomberg reported that the famous manager of a $24b. hedge fund said in a letter to clients, "Either scenario... asteroids hitting the earth or a major solar storm that could bring down the power grid...is more likely to happen than...deflation...." The degree of certainty on this issue is virtually absolute throughout the economics profession.

We'll see about that.

Anyone challenging virtually the entire army of financial and economic thinkers, from academic to professional, from liberal to conservative, from Keynesian socialist to Objectivist free-market, from Monetarist technocratic even to many vocal proponents of the Austrian school, must respond to their belief that because the Fed exists inflation is virtually inevitable and deflation impossible.

Chapter 10:

Can the Fed Stop Deflation?

"Pay no attention to that man behind the curtain."

—*The Wizard of Oz*

The primary basis for today's belief in perpetual prosperity and inflation with *perhaps* an occasional recession is what I call the "potent directors" fallacy. It is nearly impossible to find a treatise on macroeconomics today that does not assert or assume that the Federal Reserve Board has learned to control the credit supply, interest rates, the rate of inflation and the economy. Many people believe that it also possesses immense power to manipulate the stock market.

The very idea that it *can* do these things is false. Chapter 3 of *The Socionomic Theory of Finance* demonstrates unequivocally that central banks around the world *follow* prevailing interest rates; they do not set them. In 2001, before the House and Senate Joint Economic committee, Chairman Alan Greenspan himself called the idea that the Fed could prevent recessions a "puzzling" notion, chalking up such events to exactly what causes them: "human psychology." In August 1999, echoing Keynes, he more specifically described the stock market as being driven by "waves of optimism and pessimism." According to socionomic theory, he's right on this point. But no one is listening.

The Chairman also expressed the view that the Fed has the power to temper economic swings for the better. Is that what it does? Politicians and most economists assert that a central bank is necessary for maximum growth. Is that the case?

This is not the place for a treatise on the subject, but a brief dose of reality should serve. Real economic growth in the U.S. was greater in the nineteenth century without a central bank than it has been in the twentieth century with one. Real economic growth in Hong Kong during the latter half of the twentieth century outstripped that of every other country in the entire world, and it had no central bank. Anyone who advocates a causal connection between central banking and economic performance must conclude from these remarkable facts that a central bank is harmful to economic growth. For recent examples of the failure of the idea of efficacious economic directors, just look around. Since Japan's boom ended in 1990, its regulators have been using every presumed macroeconomic "tool" to get the Land of the Sinking Sun rising again, as yet to little avail. The World Bank, the IMF, local central banks and government officials were "wisely managing" Southeast Asia's boom until it collapsed spectacularly in 1997. Prevent the bust? They expressed profound dismay that it even happened. In 2007-2009, the U.S. economy imploded despite unprecedented activity by presumed "potent directors." I say "despite," but the truth is that directors *cannot* make things better and have *always* made things worse. It is a principle that meddling in the free market can only disable it. People think that the Fed has "managed" the economy brilliantly. Most financial professionals believe that the only potential culprit of a deviation from the path to ever greater prosperity would be current-time central bank actions so flagrantly stupid as to be beyond the realm of possibility. But the deep flaws in the Fed's manipulation of the banking system to facilitate the extension of credit will bear bitter fruit in the next depression. Economists who do not believe that a prolonged expansionary credit policy has consequences will soon be blasting the Fed for "mistakes" in the present, whereas the errors that matter most reside in the past. Regardless of whether this truth comes to light, the populace will disrespect the Fed and other central banks mightily by the time the depression is over. For many people, the single biggest financial shock and surprise over the next decade will be the revelation that the Fed has never really known what on earth it was doing. The spectacle of U.S. officials in 2002 lecturing Japan on how to contain deflation will be revealed as the grossest hubris. Make sure that you avoid the disillusion and financial devastation that will afflict those who harbor a misguided faith in the world's central bankers and the idea that they can manage our money, our credit or our economy.

Five Myths of Central Banking

To understand some of the reasons why I'm not snowed by the power of central bankers, I will present what I believe to be five myths of central banking.

Number 1: "The Fed will drop money from helicopters."

Former Chairman Ben Bernanke told us he would do this. But what did he mean, really? Fed employees are not physically going to climb into helicopters and disperse money like so many leaflets. He presumably meant they would buy up all the bad debts in the world. *But they haven't been doing that.*

In August 2007, at a stock market high, before the latest crisis, *The Elliott Wave Theorist* outlined the way I thought the Fed would behave:

> In the early 1930s, the Fed offered loans only on the most pristine debt. Its standards have fallen a bit, but not by much. Today it will still lend only on highly reliable IOUs, not junk. One might imagine various schemes by which the government would guarantee some mortgages, but if it did, the mortgages would in effect become Treasury bonds.

During its initial buying spree in 2008, the Fed did buy almost anything to try to save the system. But it immediately went back to its usual way. The Fed exchanged all its newly acquired weak assets for government-guaranteed mortgages, which are, in effect, Treasury bonds. In its most aggressive program, administered from 2012 to 2014, it purchased more Treasury bonds, and then government-guaranteed mortgages. Thereafter it was more Treasury bonds.

What the Fed has always done, and is still doing, is to buy U.S. Treasury bonds, which are among the safest assets in the world. It's not going around to banks teetering on the brink of failure to assure them, "We'll take all your bad stuff." The Fed doesn't want to own bad mortgages and failing business loans. In fact, it has been buying government-guaranteed mortgages *of only the most recent vintages*, meaning that they are post-crisis mortgages, which have better collateral and a much better chance of being paid off. The Fed's members are bankers; they don't want their bank to fail.

Number 2: "Central banks will just print money."

This is a nearly universal belief, especially among people who expect hyperinflation. But tell this fable to the people who live in Cyprus. Losses in Cypriot banks in 2013 were estimated to be as high as 60%. That's a systemic banking failure. Were depositors rescued? Read this news report from 2013: "A weekend agreement between Cyprus and its European partners called for the government to *raid bank accounts*." To do so, authorities shut down Cyprus' second-largest bank, "imposing steep losses on deposits with more than 100,000 euros." The lenders in this case were the Eurozone, the IMF and the European Central Bank. They are supposed to be the saviors, the bailers-out. But the ECB did not print money to save these depositors. European officials said in effect, "We lent you money. We want it back. Now you pay *us*." They called the seizure a "tax" on depositors. But it was nothing more than a banking failure. Those who paid were not the central bankers but those hapless souls known euphemistically as depositors. To trap people, authorities imposed "strict controls on money transfers in and out of the economy." At air and seaports, officials were confiscating amounts over 10,000 euros. See how it works? No helicopters.

Number 3: "Central banks stand ready to be lenders of last resort."

Founders of central banks always make this promise. But in Europe we found out something very different. According to a March 25, 2013 article in *The Telegraph*, "Savings accounts in Spain, Italy and other European countries *will be raided* if needed to preserve Europe's single currency by propping up failing banks, a senior Eurozone official has announced." But raiding accounts is not "propping up failing banks"; it's just distributing the failure. The Dutch chairman of the Eurozone said — listen to this — "Look, where *you* take on risks, *you* must deal with them, and if *you* can't deal with them, then *you* shouldn't have taken them on." Notice it's not *us* but *you.*

He then said, "Banks should basically be able to *save themselves.*" Wait a minute! Didn't they used to call this policy "wildcat banking," whereby a bank was responsible for its own health and depositors paid for failures? It seems we're back to square one! But we're not; we're way worse off. In the old days, when one bank failed, one bank failed. Under central banking, debt is socialized, so failures become systemic.

Surprise: There's no free lunch. Not only did central bankers not ride to the rescue of weak European banks in 2013 but they also decided on "mothballing the 700 billion Euro bailout fund, the European Stability Mechanism (ESM)." Of course they did. Infinite credit works only in theory.

Consider the psychology of these lenders. They abandoned the expansionary attitudes they held for over a decade. Instead, they worried, "Maybe we won't get paid later; we'd better get paid today." By acting to protect themselves, they were thinking in a deflationary manner, just like the rest of society.

Number 4: "Inflation is determined by the expansion of base money."

Many people have been saying that the Fed's QE programs guarantee hyperinflation. But inflation is a net expansion of money *and credit.* Usually an episode of deflation is a swift

Inflation is the net expansion of money + **credit**
Base-money dollars: **$4.5t.**
Dollar denominated debt: **$68.6t.** U.S. bank deposits: **$12t.** Federal unfunded liabilities: **$112t.** total: **$192.6t.**
Additional global debt: **$233t.*** Global unfunded liabilities: **$200t.**? total: **$433t.**
Global derivatives: **$542t.-1.2 quadrillion**
Total: **$1.17-1.83 quadrillion****
*Only $4t. of global debt (2%) is rated AAA **less than 0.4% of the total is base-money dollars

Figure 10-1

contraction in credit, not base money. With that understanding, let's look at the potential for credit deflation, as summarized in Figure 10-1.

Base money, produced by the Fed, has risen to $4.5 trillion. That is a tremendous amount of money. But relative to the amount of dollars owed, it's still pretty small. Dollar denominated debt is $68.6 trillion. U.S. bank deposits amount to $12 trillion. These are all IOUs; most of the money's not there; it's been lent. Estimates of federal unfunded liabilities range from $474t. to $210t.; the U.S. debt clock website estimates $112t. That's a total of about $193 trillion worth of IOUs. The base of $4.5 trillion doesn't look so big when compared to that number.

Globally, there is an additional $233 trillion worth of debt. Total unfunded liabilities, I'm guessing, amount to around $200 trillion, for a total of $433 trillion.

This figure doesn't take into account global financial derivatives. Estimates range substantially. As of June 30, 2017, the official Bank of International Settlements' figure for total notational value of OTC derivatives is $542 trillion, but off-the-books "shadow" derivatives valued at $650 trillion raise Investopedia's latest high-end approximation to $1.2 quadrillion. Current market value for all these derivatives is as little as 2% of the notional value, but what matters is how much debt these promises will represent in a financial crisis, not a benign environment such as exists today. I call derivatives "IOU-if's." They're not IOUs now, but if certain events were to happen they would *turn into* IOUs. That's a lot of potential new debt. So, total debt plus potential debt is somewhere north of a quadrillion dollars' worth, making $4.5 trillion not seem like a whole lot. In fact, it is less than 0.45% of the total.

Moreover, consider that only $4 trillion worth of total global debt is AAA. That's only 2%; 98% of the debt is graded lower. This fact portends a slew of defaults from even a modest rise in interest rates coupled with an economic contraction.

Number 5: "The Fed's Inflating Will Change People's Psychology"

The Fed's actions cannot change people's psychology. On the contrary, people's psychology prompts actions by the Fed. Chapter 28 of *The Socionomic Theory of Finance* offers a hilarious demonstration of this fact

Figure 10-2 shows very clearly that since 1997-2000, subtly waxing deflationary psychology has hindered the Fed's drive to inflate. Money velocity — the rate at which money changes hands — tends to rise when social mood is trending positively and economic activity is expanding, and fall when mood is trending negatively and the economy is contracting. It has a long history of reversing and retreating years before major tops in the stock market, thereby providing an advance warning of major bear markets and depressions. Examine the chart action between 1918, near the peak the commodity boom of a century ago, and 1929,

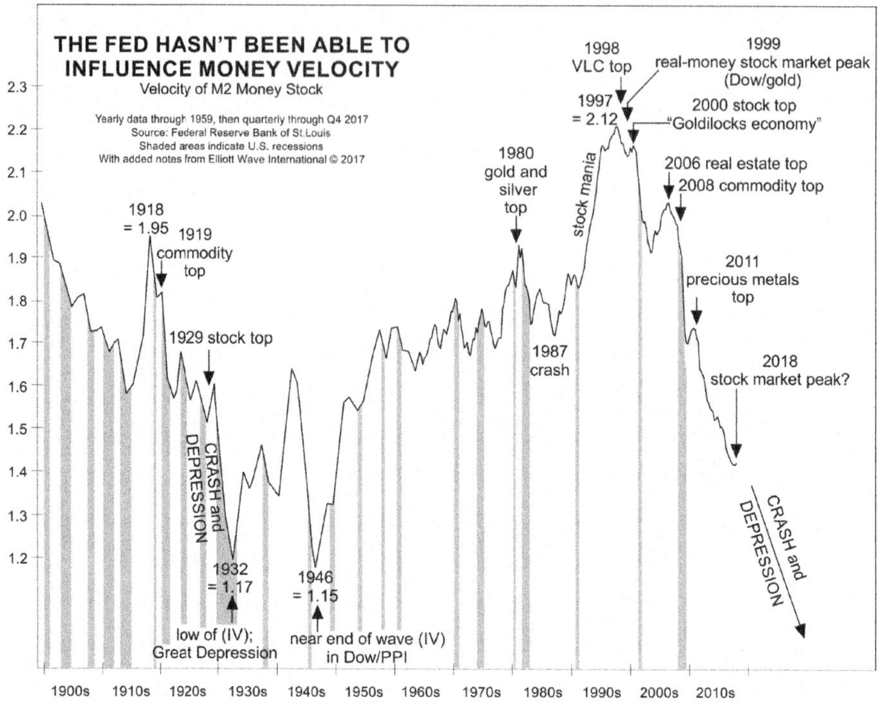

Figure 10-2

when stocks made a Supercycle-degree top. Simply stated, money velocity fell for eleven years before the stock market crashed and depression set in. That history appears to be repeating but on a larger scale. As you can see in Figure 10-2, money velocity in the U.S. peaked in the third quarter of 1997 and has been slackening ever since. The only significant bounce along the way is the one that accompanied the final three years of the real-estate mania from 2003 into the second quarter of 2006. From there, money velocity plunged along with all financial markets into the second quarter of 2009, when the Great Recession ended. A weak bounce into Q3 2010 accompanied most of the final wave of advance in the ten-year bull market for silver and gold, which peaked in April and September 2011, respectively. Since that time, in the face of the continuing bull market in stocks and a moderate but persistent expansion in the economy, *money velocity has been making new lows quarter after quarter.* It has had but two negligible one-quarter bounces, the most recent being that of Q4 2017, as nominal stock prices became historically high.

Changes in money velocity are a psychological phenomenon, not a mechanical one. Sliding velocity in 2008 was a big reason why the Fed had to resort to inflating the base money supply. The Fed has been expecting its QE programs to force velocity back up, but so far it hasn't. On the contrary, the fall in money turnover has persisted throughout the Fed's most aggressively inflationary monetary policy ever, the nearly $4 trillion expansion that ran from 2008 through 2014. That unprecendented policy was so ineffective that it failed to stop real estate, commodities and precious metals from having huge bear markets, even in *nominal* terms. It has now been not eleven but *twenty* years since money velocity peaked. Today's stock market top is one degree higher than that of 1929, and the setup indicated by Figure 10-2 supports that case.

Hubristic macro-directors will be unable to fend off the approaching tide of negative social mood, which, like its positive cousin, will derive from unconscious human impulses. The dichotomy between falling money velocity and rising stock prices seems to be approaching a standstill. But a winner will emerge. When social mood turns toward the negative again, velocity will fall even further, credit will shrink, the stock market will fall, and the economy will contract. Induced inflation, by whatever authority, will prove inadequate to the task of reversing those trends.

Monetary Models Ignore Psychology

Conventional economists today are in virtually unanimous agreement that the Fed can stop any trend toward deflation and economic contraction. Even the experience of 2008—in which the Fed failed to prevent a breathtaking collapse in credit and the deepest recession in 75 years—has not deterred professionals' faith in the Fed's power. Such faith is nearly as old as the Fed itself. On

October 19, 1929, as the U.S. stock market was beginning its most famous crash to date, the Harvard Economic Society, populated by the most intelligent economists in the nation, issued this confident statement: "If recession should threaten serious consequences for business (as is not indicated at present) there is little doubt that the Reserve System would take steps to ease the money market and so check the movement" (Frederick Lewis Allen, *Only Yesterday*, 1931). Simple, right? Yes, and simplistic, not to mention dead wrong. This naïve belief in the Fed's "policy levers," even more prevalent today, is based on the false paradigm of social mechanics, which in turn is due not to a reliable body of evidence but to an unconscious default in the human mind. (See *The Socionomic Theory of Finance*, 2016.) The central problem is that modern monetary theorists don't take into account the active (as opposed to reactive) psychology of human beings. Yet this is the very factor that ruins their neat models. They think governments and central banks need only to pull on levers to make things happen. But when people suddenly get angry, fearful and defensive, the entire situation changes. Their neat lab becomes a circus. Only socionomists understand the primacy of social mood to all things financial. Waves of social mood, we say, bring about waves of social change.

In 1929, the party was on, and no one could envision how dramatically things would change. Just three years later, banks were failing across the country and unemployment was pushing 25% in the deepest depression since the late 1700s.

In 1937, people were celebrating the economic recovery and dancing to Benny Goodman. No one had a clue as to how different the world would soon become. In just three years, Hitler's tanks were raging through Europe, people were being rounded up for shipment to concentration camps, Japan joined the Axis, and World War II was raging.

Conversely, in 1942, the market had sunk to its lowest price/earnings (P/E) ratio ever, Japan had wiped out U.S. naval ships at Pearl Harbor, and Germany was winning the war in Europe. That's when R.N. Elliott published a chart predicting 70 years of rising stock prices. He was right, and prosperity and peace followed.

Today, the market is at an extreme in the other direction. Psychology will change, and social events will follow, no matter what the Fed does. Ironically, the deeply held faith in the power of the Fed is one of the mindsets that will lead countless economists and their followers to slaughter in the next crisis.

The Fed used to have three supposed sources of power to facilitate the expansion of bank credit: It could lower reserve requirements; it could lower the discount rate, the rate at which it lends money to banks; and it could monetize debt, a process now called "quantitative easing." In shepherding reserve requirements down to zero, te Fed has expended all the presumed power of the first source. In 2008, the Fed followed the market in lowering its discount rate all the way to zero, thereby expending all the presumed power of the second source. It was lucky the economy stopped contracting after a Great Recession rather than having continued on to a Great Depression. The next contraction will not be so accommodating. What about QE? Is that a trump card?

Why the Fed Cannot Stop Deflation

Countless people say that deflation is impossible because the Fed can just *print money* to stave off deflation. If the Fed's main jobs were simply establishing new checking accounts and grinding out banknotes, that's what it might do. But in terms of *volume*, that has not been the Fed's primary function, which for 104 years has been in fact to foster the *expansion of credit*. Printed fiat currency depends almost entirely upon the whims of the issuer, but credit is another matter entirely.

What the Fed does is to try to influence certain very short-term interbank loan rates called federal funds. It sets the discount rate, which is the Fed's nominal near-term lending rate to banks. Then it buys and sells overnight "repurchase agreements," which are collateralized loans among banks and dealers, to defend its virtually irrelevant "target" for the federal funds rate. In stable times, the lower the rate at which banks can borrow short-term funds, the lower the rate at which they can offer long-term loans to the public. Thus, though the Fed undertakes its operations to influence bank borrowing, its ultimate goal is to influence public borrowing from banks. Observe that the Fed makes bank credit more available or less available to two sets of *willing borrowers.*

During trends toward positive social mood, this strategy appears to work, because the borrowers — i.e., banks and their customers — are confident, eager participants in the process. During monetary crises, the Fed's attempts to target interest rates don't appear to work because in such environments, the demands of creditors overwhelm the Fed's desires. In the inflationary 1970s to early 1980s, rates of interest soared to 16%, and the Fed was forced to follow, not because it wanted that interest rate but because creditors demanded it.

Regardless of the discount and federal funds rates, banks set their own lending rates to customers. During economic contractions, banks can become fearful to make long-term loans even with cheap short-term money. In that case, they raise their loan rates to make up for the perceived risk of loss. In particularly scary times, banks have been known virtually to cease new commercial, real estate and consumer lending altogether, as happened in 2008-2012. Thus, the ultimate success of the Fed's attempts to lower interest rates depends not only upon willing borrowers but also upon the banks as *willing creditors.*

Economists hint at the Fed's occasional impotence in fostering credit expansion when they describe an ineffective monetary strategy, i.e., a drop in the Fed's target rate that does not stimulate borrowing, as "pushing on a string." At such times, low Fed-influenced rates cannot overcome creditors' disinclination to lend and/or customers' unwillingness or inability to borrow. When prices for goods fall rapidly during a deflationary episode, the value of money rises, so even a zero interest rate imposes a heavy real cost on borrowers, who are obligated to return more valuable dollars at a later date. Some interest rates have gone negative in recent years, but there is a limit to that trend, which is the amount of premium savers are willing to pay for the transactional convenience of holding a money-losing bond or bank account vs. holding currency notes.

When banks and investors are reluctant to lend, only *higher* interest rates can induce them to do so. In deflationary times, the market accommodates this pressure with falling bond prices and higher lending rates for all but the most pristine debtors. But wait; it's not that simple, because higher interest rates do not serve only to *attract* capital; they can also make it flee. Once again, the determinant of the difference is market psychology. Creditors in a defensive frame of mind can perceive a borrower's willingness to pay high rates as desperation, in which case, the higher the offer, the more repelled is the creditor. In a deflationary crash, rising interest rates on bonds mean that creditors fear default.

A defensive credit market can scuttle the Fed's efforts to get lenders and borrowers to agree to transact at all, much less at some desired target rate. If people and corporations are unwilling to borrow or unable to finance debt, and if banks and investors are disinclined to lend, central banks cannot force them to do so. During deflation, they cannot even induce them to do so with a zero interest rate.

Thus, regardless of assertions to the contrary, the Fed's purported "control" of borrowing, lending and interest rates ultimately depends upon accommodating market psychology and cannot be set by decree. So, ultimately, the Fed does not control either interest rates or the total supply of credit; the market does.

There is an invisible group of lenders in the money game: *complacent depositors*, who — thanks to the FDIC (see Chapter 16) and their own ignorance of the risk — have been letting banks engage in whatever lending activities they like. Depositors might become highly skittish (if not horrified) if they knew how their money is being handled.

In contrast to the assumptions of conventional macroeconomic models, people are not machines. They get emotional. People become depressed, fearful, cautious and angry during depressions; that's essentially what causes them. A change in the population's mental state from a desire to expand to a desire to conserve is key to understanding why central bank machinations cannot avert deflation.

When ebullience makes people expansive, they often act on impulse, without full regard to reason. That's why, for example, consumers, corporations and governments can allow themselves to take on huge masses of debt, an action they later regret. It is why creditors can be comfortable lending to weak borrowers, a decision they later regret. It is also why stocks can reach unprecedented valuations.

Conversely, when fear makes people defensive, they again often act on impulse, without full regard to reason. An example of a type of action impelled by defensive psychology is the increasing conservatism of bankers during a credit contraction. When lending officers become afraid, they call in loans and slow or stop their lending no matter how good their clients' credit may be, as happened in 2008-2012. Instead of seeing opportunity, they see only danger. Ironically, much of the actual danger appears as a consequence of the reckless, impulsive decisions that they made in the preceding uptrend. In an environment of pessimism, corporations likewise reduce borrowing for expansion and acquisition, fearing the burden more than they believe in the opportunity. Consumers adopt a defensive strategy at such times by opting to save and conserve rather than to borrow and spend. Anything the Fed does in such a climate will be seen through the lens of cynicism and fear. In such a mental state, people will interpret Fed actions differently from the way that they did when they were inclined toward confidence and hope.

With these thoughts in mind, let's return to the idea that the Fed could just print banknotes to stave off bank failures. One can imagine a scenario in which the Fed, beginning soon after the onset of deflation, trades banknotes for portfolios of bad loans, replacing a sea of bad debt with an equal ocean of banknotes, thus smoothly monetizing all defaults in the system without a ripple of protest, reaction or deflation.

There are two problems with this scenario. One is that the Fed is a bank, and it would have no desire to go broke buying up worthless portfolios, debasing the value of its own reserves to nothing. Only a government mandate triggered by crisis could compel such an action, which would come only after deflation had ravaged the system. Even in 1933, when the Fed agreed to monetize some banks' loans, it offered cash in exchange for only the very best loans in the banks' portfolios, not the precarious ones. Second, the smooth reflation scenario is an ivory-tower concoction that sounds plausible only by omitting human beings from it. While the Fed could embark on an aggressive plan to liquefy the banking system with cash in response to a developing credit crisis, that action itself ironically could serve to aggravate deflation, not relieve it. In a defensive emotional environment, evidence that the Fed or the government had decided to adopt a deliberate policy of inflating the currency could give bondholders an excuse, justified or not, to panic. It could be taken as evidence that the crisis is worse than they thought, which would make them fear defaults among borrowers, or that hyperinflation lay ahead, which could make them fear the depreciation of all dollar-denominated debt. Nervous holders of debt that was near expiration could simply decline to exercise their option to repurchase it once the current holding term ran out. Fearful holders of long-term debt far from expiration could dump their notes and bonds on the market, making prices collapse. If this were to happen, the net result of an attempt at inflating would be a system-wide reduction in the purchasing power of dollar-denominated debt, in other words, a drop in the dollar value of total credit extended, which is deflation. The bond market therefore stands ready to dissolve the myth of Fed's omnipotence.

With today's full disclosure of central banks' activities, governments and central banks cannot hide their monetary decisions. Indications that the Fed had adopted an unwelcome policy would spread immediately around the world, and the bond market would adjust accordingly. Downward adjustments in bond prices could not only negate but also *outrun* the Fed's attempts at money expansion.

The problems that the Fed faces are due to the fact that the world is not so much awash in money as it is awash in credit. Because today the quantity of credit dwarfs the quantity of money, debt investors, who always have the option to sell bonds in large quantities, are in the driver's seat with respect to interest rates, currency values and the total quantity of credit, which means that they, not the Fed, are in charge of the prospects for inflation and deflation. The Fed has become a slave to trends that it has already fostered for over a hundred years, to events that have already transpired. For the Fed, the mass of credit that it has nursed into the world is like having raised King Kong from babyhood as a pet. He might behave, but only if you can figure out what he wants and keep him satisfied.

In the context of our discussion, the Fed has four relevant tasks: to keep the banking system liquid, to maintain the public's confidence in banks, to maintain the market's faith in the value of Treasury securities, which constitute its own reserves, and to maintain the integrity of the dollar relative to other currencies, since the dollar is still the world's reserve currency, which affords the Fed and the U.S. government substantial power. In a system-wide financial crisis, these goals will conflict. If the Fed chooses to favor any one of these goals, the others will be at least compromised, possibly doomed.

The Fed may have taken its steps to eliminate reserve requirements with these conflicts in mind, because whether by unintended consequence or design, that regulatory change transferred the full moral responsibility for depositors' money onto the banks. The Fed has thus excused itself from responsibility in a system-wide banking crisis, giving itself the option of defending the dollar or the Treasury's debt rather than your bank deposits. Indeed, from 1928 to 1933, the Fed raised its holdings of Treasury securities from 10.8% of its credit portfolio to 91.5%, effectively "fleeing to quality" right along with the rest of the market. What actual path the Fed will take under pressure is unknown, but it is important to know that it is under no *obligation* to save the banks, print money or pursue any other rescue. Its primary legal obligation is to provide backing for the nation's currency, which it could quite merrily fulfill no matter what happens to the banking system.

Local Inflation by Repatriation?

Other countries hold Treasury securities in their central banks as reserves, and their citizens keep dollar bills as a store of value and medium of exchange. In fact, foreigners hold 42.5% of the Treasury securities in the marketplace and 75% of all $100 bills. Repatriation of those instruments, it has been proposed, could cause a dramatic local inflation. If investors around the world were to panic over prospects for dollar hyperinflation, that very panic would cause a collapse in prices for Treasury securities, which would be deflationary. If credit were deflating faster than money was inflating, dollar bills would rise in value over that period of time. Foreigners would want to hold onto those remaining dollar bills with both hands. Even if foreign banks were to return masses of dollars to the Fed, the Fed, as required by law, would have to swap Treasury bonds for the returned currency, thus neutralizing the monetary effect. That hoardes of dollar-holders would swap money back to the U.S. is a fanciful idea, anyway. All they would do in real life is spend them locally, like everyone else.

Can Fiscal Policy Halt Deflation?

Can the government spend its way out of deflation and depression? Governments sometimes employ aspects of "fiscal policy," i.e., altering spending or taxing activities, to "pump up" demand for goods and services. Raising taxes for any reason would be harmful. Increasing government spending (with or without raising taxes) simply transfers wealth from savers to spenders, substituting a short-run stimulus for long-run economic deterioration. Japan has used this approach for years, and it hasn't worked. Slashing taxes absent government spending cuts would be useless because the government would have to borrow the difference. Cutting government spending is a good thing, but politics will prevent its happening prior to a crisis.

Understand further that even the government's "tools" of macroeconomic manipulation are hardly mechanical levers on a machine; they are subject to the psychology of the manipulators. A sea change in *thinking* is what ultimately causes trends such as inflation and deflation, and it can happen to central bankers, too.

Endgame

The lack of solutions to the deflation problem is due to the fact that the problem results from prior excesses. Like the discomfort of drug addiction withdrawal, the discomfort of credit addiction withdrawal cannot be avoided. The time to have thought about avoiding a system-wide deflation was years ago. Now it's too late.

It does not matter how it happens; in the right psychological environment, *deflation will win*. People today, raised in the benign, expansive environment of a multi-decade bull market, love to quote the conventional wisdom, "Don't fight the Fed." Now that the environment is about to change, I think that the cry of the truly wise should be, "Don't fight the waves."

Currency Hyperinflation

While I can discern no obvious forces that would counteract deflation, *after* deflation is another matter. At the bottom, when there is little credit left to destroy, currency inflation, perhaps even hyperinflation, could come into play.

When a government embarks on a policy of currency hyperinflation, such as the Confederate States did in the 1860s, Germany did in the early 1920s or France did after World War II, the monetary path and end result are different from those of deflation.

At the end of hyperinflation, every bank account denominated in the hyperinflated currency is worthless; all debts disappear, because the notes are denominated in worthless money; and even the money disappears. Therefore, with deflation, the end result is the destruction of credit and the elevation of money, whereas with hyperinflation, the end result is the destruction of both credit *and* money, a far worse outcome.

The Markets Will Signal Inflation

Despite my thoughts on the matter, I recognize that international money flows are massive, central bankers can be ingenious, and politics can be volatile. Perhaps there is some way that inflation, whether globally or locally, could accelerate during the crisis. How can you tell if my conclusion about deflation is wrong and that inflation or hyperinflation is taking place *instead* of deflation?

There are three sensitive barometers of major monetary trends: the foreign currency market, interest rates and gold prices. If *all three* rise simultaneously, the U.S. dollar will be experiencing inflation. Singly, they might mean something else. If the price of the dollar against other currencies begins to plummet, it might simply mean that credit denominated in other currencies is deflating faster than that denominated in dollars. If interest rates rise, it might simply mean that investors fear default. Even gold can rise absent accelerating inflation, as happened from 2001 to 2011. To be sure of hyperinflation, all three markets must be moving up at once.

This book attempts to outline some of the longer-term risks and suggests ways to deal with them. Yet despite best efforts, it may not have all the answers.

Part III

How to Protect Yourself and Profit from Deflation and Depression

"...but Philamis...followed his ould course...thinking that the tide would have no ebb, the tune would have no ende."

— Thomas Lodge, *Euphues' Shadowe* (1592)

For Your Safety

If present or future laws pertaining to the reader prohibit any financial or other activity suggested in this book, the reader is advised to consider any contrary suggestion null and void and proceed according to applicable law. Neither the author nor the publisher acts as portfolio manager, securities advisor, trading advisor, attorney, underwriter, solicitor or broker. At no time does the author or publisher advocate any particular reader's acquisition of any specific financial product or service. If you require personalized advice, you should seek the services of a competent professional.

Chapter 11:

Making Preparations and Taking Action

The ultimate effect of deflation is to reduce the supply of credit, which totally serves as most people's money. Your goal is to make sure that it doesn't reduce the supply of *your* credit and money. The ultimate effect of depression is financial ruin. Your goal is to make sure that it doesn't ruin you.

Many investment advisors speak as if making money by investing is easy. It's not. What's easy is *losing* money, which is exactly what most investors do. They might make money for a while, but they lose eventually. Just keeping what you have over a lifetime of investing can be an achievement. That's what this book is designed to help you do, in perhaps the single most difficult financial environment that exists.

Protecting your liquid wealth against a deflationary crash and depression is pretty easy once you know what to do. Protecting your other assets and ensuring your livelihood can be serious challenges. Knowing how to proceed used to be the most difficult part of your task because almost no one writes about the issue. This book remedies that situation.

Preparing To Take the Right Actions

In a crash and depression, we will see asset values go down 90% or more, massive layoffs, high unemployment, corporate and municipal bankruptcies, pension fund implosions, bank and insurance company failures and ultimately financial and political crises. The average person, who has no inkling of the risks in the financial system, will be shocked that such things could happen, despite the fact that they have happened repeatedly throughout history.

Being unprepared will leave you vulnerable to a major disruption in your life. Being prepared will allow you to make exceptional profits both in the crash and in the ensuing recovery. For now, you should focus on making sure that you do not become a zombie-eyed victim of the depression.

The best news of all is that this depression should be relatively brief, though it will seem like an eternity while it is in force. The longest depression on record in the U.S. lasted three years and five months, from September 1929 to February 1933. The longest sustained stock market decline in U.S. history—which led to depression—lasted seven years, from 1835 to 1842. A second depression occurred in the late 1850s. As the expected trend change is of one larger degree than those, it should be a commensurately large setback, but it should still be brief relative to the duration of the preceding advance.

Taking the Right Actions

Countless advisors have counseled "diversification," a "balanced portfolio" and other end-all solutions to the problem of allocating your investments. These approaches are usually delusions. As I try to make clear in the following pages, no investment strategy will provide stability *forever*. You will have to be nimble enough to see major trends coming and make changes accordingly. What follows is a good guide, I think, but it is only a guide.

The main goal of investing in a crash environment is *safety*. When deflation looms, almost every investment category becomes associated with immense risks. Most investors have no idea of these risks and will think you are a fool for taking precautions.

Many readers will object to taking certain prudent actions because of the presumed cost. For example: "I can't take a profit; I'll have to pay taxes!" My reply is, if you don't want to pay taxes,

What's *that* for?

well, you'll get your wish; your profit will turn into a loss, and you won't have to pay any taxes. Or they say, "I can't sell my stocks for cash; interest rates are only 2½%!" My reply is, if you can't abide a 2½% annual gain, well, you'll get your wish there, too; you'll have a 30% annual loss instead. Others say, "I can't cash out my retirement plan; there's a penalty!" I reply, take your money out before there is none to get. Then there is the venerable, "I can't sell now; I'd be taking a loss!" I say no, you are recovering some capital that you can put to better use. My advice always is, make the right move, and the costs will take care of themselves.

If you are preoccupied with pedestrian concerns or blithely going along with mainstream opinions, you need to wake up now, while there is still time, and actively take charge of your personal finances. First you must make your capital, your person and your family safe. Then you can explore options for making money during the crash and especially after it's over.

As its subtitle implies, this book is designed as a guide for arranging your finances prior to any future deflationary depression, whether one occurs now, as I expect, or not. Although I want this book to have value beyond the present situation, some of the specifics of my suggestions are time-sensitive by nature. If you need to know today where you can find the few exceptionally sound banks and other essential service providers, if you want to locate the safest structures in the world for storing your wealth, whether in paper monetary instruments or physical assets such as precious metals, you will find the answers in these chapters. Yet over time, the best institutions and services of today might be long gone, and others may have taken their place. You may have to do your own research. Nevertheless, the general nature of your goals — even 300 years from now — should be much as outlined herein.

Most people do not have the foggiest idea how to prepare their portfolios for a deflationary crash and depression, so the techniques are almost like secrets today. The following chapters show you a few steps that will make your finances secure despite almost anything that such an environment can throw at them.

Chapter 12:

Should You Invest in Bonds?

If there is one bit of conventional wisdom that we hear repeatedly with respect to investing for a deflationary depression, it is that long-term bonds are the best possible investment. This assertion is wrong. Any bond issued by a borrower who cannot pay goes to *zero* in a depression. In the Great Depression, bonds of many companies, municipalities and foreign governments were crushed. Some became wallpaper as their issuers went bankrupt and defaulted. Bonds of *suspect* issuers also went way down, at least for a time. Understand that in a crash, no one knows its depth, and almost everyone becomes afraid. Fear and uncertainty prompt investors to sell bonds of any issuers that they fear could default. Even when people trust the bonds they own, they are sometimes forced to sell them to raise cash to live on. For this reason, even the safest bonds can go down, at least temporarily, as AAA bonds did in 1931 and 1932.

Figure 12-1 shows what happened to bonds of various grades in the last deflationary crash. Figure 12-2 shows what happened to the Dow Jones 40-bond average, which lost 30% of its value in four years. Observe that the collapse of the early 1930s brought these bonds' prices *below* — and their interest rates above — where they were in 1920 near the peak in the intense inflation of the 'Teens. Figure 12-3 shows a comparable data series (the Bond Buyer 20-Bond average) in recent decades. Notice how similar

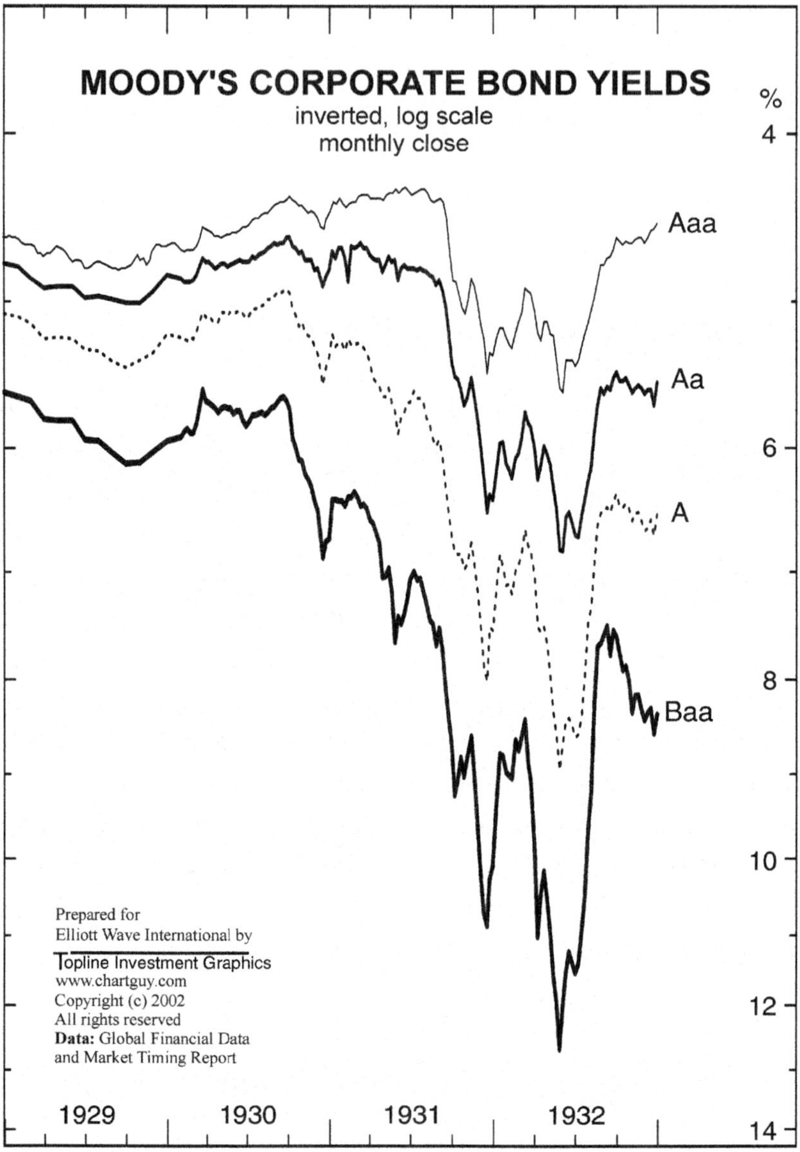
MOODY'S CORPORATE BOND YIELDS
inverted, log scale
monthly close
%
4
6
8
10
12
14
Aaa
Aa
A
Baa
1929
1930
1931
1932
Prepared for
Elliott Wave International by
Topline Investment Graphics
www.chartguy.com
Copyright (c) 2002
All rights reserved
Data: Global Financial Data
and Market Timing Report

Figure 12-1

the pattern is to that of 1915-1929. If bonds follow the path that they did in the 1930s, their prices will fall *below the 1981 low, and their interest rates will exceed that year's peak of 16%.*

Conventional analysts who have not studied the Great Depression or who expect bonds to move contra-cyclically to stocks

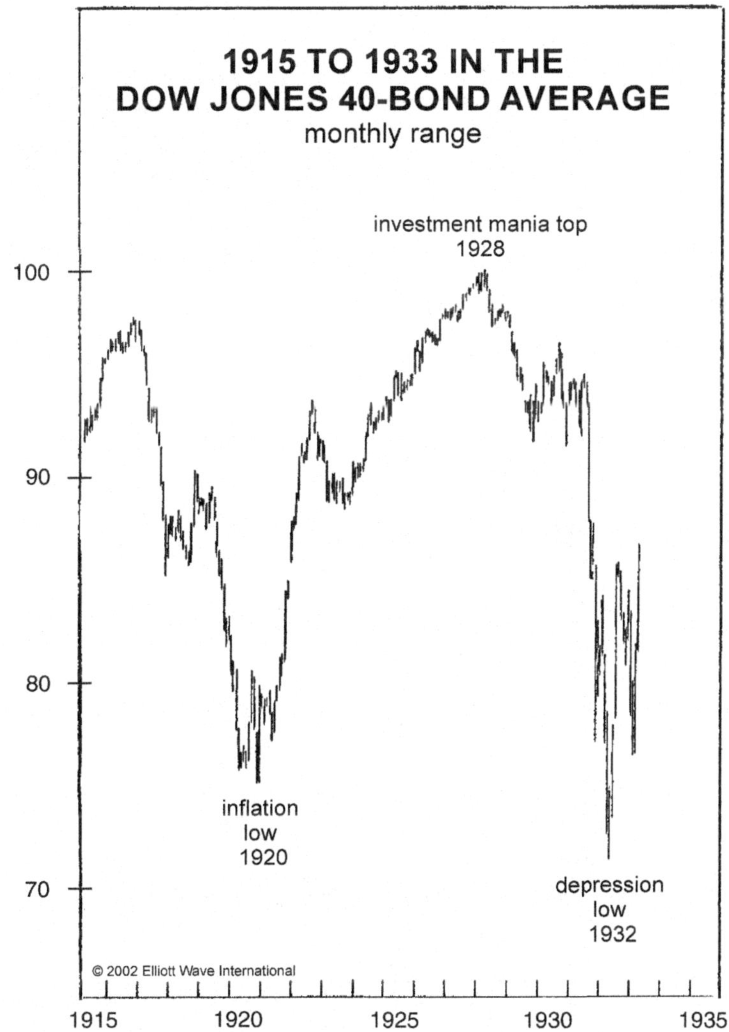

Figure 12-2

are going to be shocked to see their bonds plummeting in value right along with the stock market. Ironically, economists will see the first wave down in bonds as a sign of inflation and a strong economy, when in fact, it will be the opposite.

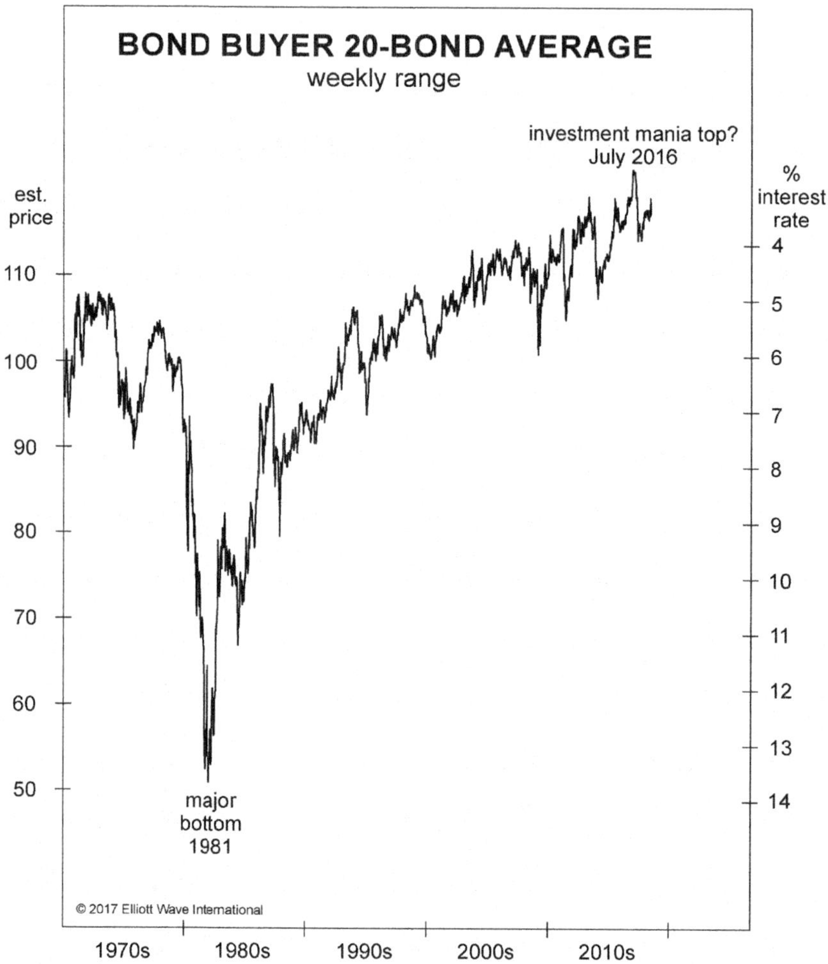

Figure 12-3

The Specter of Downgrading

The main problem with even these cautionary graphs is that they do not show the full impact of *downgrades*. They show what bonds *of a certain quality* sold for at each data point. Bonds rated AAA or BBB at the start of a depression generally do not keep those ratings throughout it. Many go straight to D and then become de-listed because of default. Figure 12-1 does not take the price devastation of these issues into account. Like keepers of stock market averages who replace the companies that fail along the way, keepers of bond averages stand ready to replace component bonds whose ratings fall too far. So, as scary as they look, these graphs fail to depict the real misery that a depression inflicts upon bond investors.

High-Yield Bonds

When rating services rate bonds between BBB and AAA, they imply that they are considered safe investments. Anything rated BB or lower is considered speculative, implying that there is a risk that the borrower someday could default. The lower the rating, the greater that risk. Because of this risk, Wall Street, in a rare display of honesty, calls bonds rated BB or lower "junk." They have "high yields," though, so people buy them.

High yields, however, compound the risk to principal. In a bad economy, issuers of high-yield bonds find it increasingly difficult to meet their interest payments. The prices of those bonds fall as investors perceive the increased risk and sell them. The ultimate result in such cases is a low or negative total return. If the issuer defaults, your principal is gone.

The Elliott Wave Theorist first recommended action in high-yield bonds on March 28, 1988. It was the first time that there was something to say about these investments, which had been valued quite consistently at "par" since they had grown from obscurity several years earlier into a multi-billion dollar market. Their yield above Treasury notes at the time was only 3.5%, reflecting a bullish complacency toward junk bonds and the economy. Here is that issue's comment on these low-grade, high-yield debt instruments:

> If you can figure out a way to short "junk" bonds, do it. This sector has rallied back to a small spread against T-bonds, and complacency is entrenched. A depression will wipe out the value of these bonds. No one reading this publication should be invested in junk bonds.

Three months later, in June, the market started down, slowly at first. In October, the slide began to accelerate. In April 1989, articles referred to junk-bond trading sessions as involving "chaos," "turmoil" and "panic." In truth, they had seen nothing yet. As you can see in Figure 12-4, the last bounce worthy of the name ended in June 1989. That was wave 2 of (3), from which point junk bond prices crashed in the "third of the third" wave. Throughout the decline, analysts were baffled because the economy was still expanding, and there was "no reason" for the fall. The market, as always, was way ahead of events. The fall in junk bond prices was a flight from low quality in anticipation of an event that in fact did

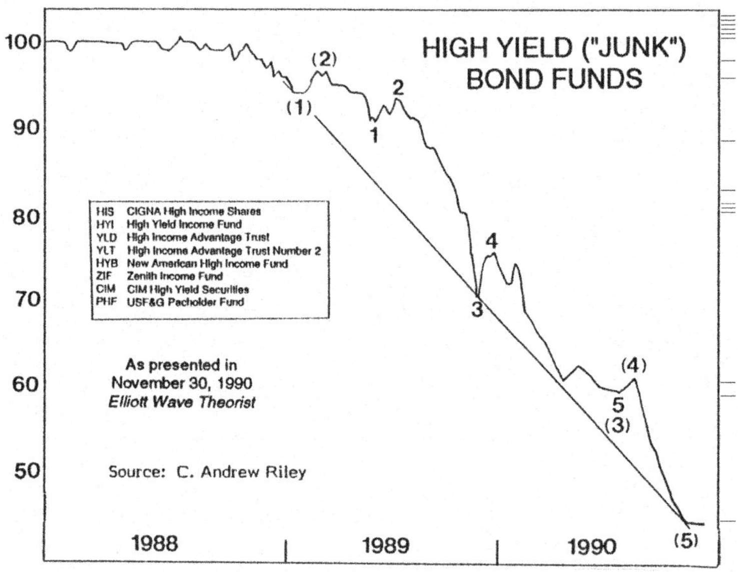

Figure 12-4

not occur until more than a year later, in the second half of 1990: a recession. *The Elliott Wave Theorist* figured out this fact a year in advance, commenting as follows in the August 18, 1989 issue:

> Many professional economists have embraced the idea of an upcoming "soft landing," i.e., that the Fed (yes, once again) has discovered the secret to avoiding recessions. The junk bond market appears to have different ideas, as the spread between its yield and that of Treasuries has continued to widen, reflecting recession worries.

Junk bonds were right that a recession was coming. Its official beginning was July 1990 and its official end was March 1991. True to the market's seemingly perverse yet perfectly logical and necessary ways, the decline in junk bonds ended in the fourth quarter of 1990, *early* in the recession, in the heat of "debt quality" downgrades by rating services (two years late), the largest dollar amount of junk bond defaults in nineteen years, and confirmation by many economists that a recession was beginning (though most argued about it for another couple of months).

The decline in junk bond prices traced out five waves down, complete with an extended third wave, that wiped out almost 60% of total junk bond values in just two short years. At the low in December 1990, the yield of the Merrill Lynch High Yield Index had soared to 17.4%, a premium of 9.3% above the 8.1% yield of ten-year Treasury notes, reflecting widespread fear.

Memorize this scenario, as it is undoubtedly in the early stages of playing out once again. Ask yourself, did investors learn anything as a result of the collapse? Did they learn anything from the crisis of 2006-2009, which — as you can see in Figure 12-5 — was equally destructive to prices for weaker debt? The answer is an unqualified "No."

In the Great Depression, interest rates on low-grade bonds trended lower until 1930, and those on high-grade bonds continued lower until 1931. Then they soared as prices plummeted.

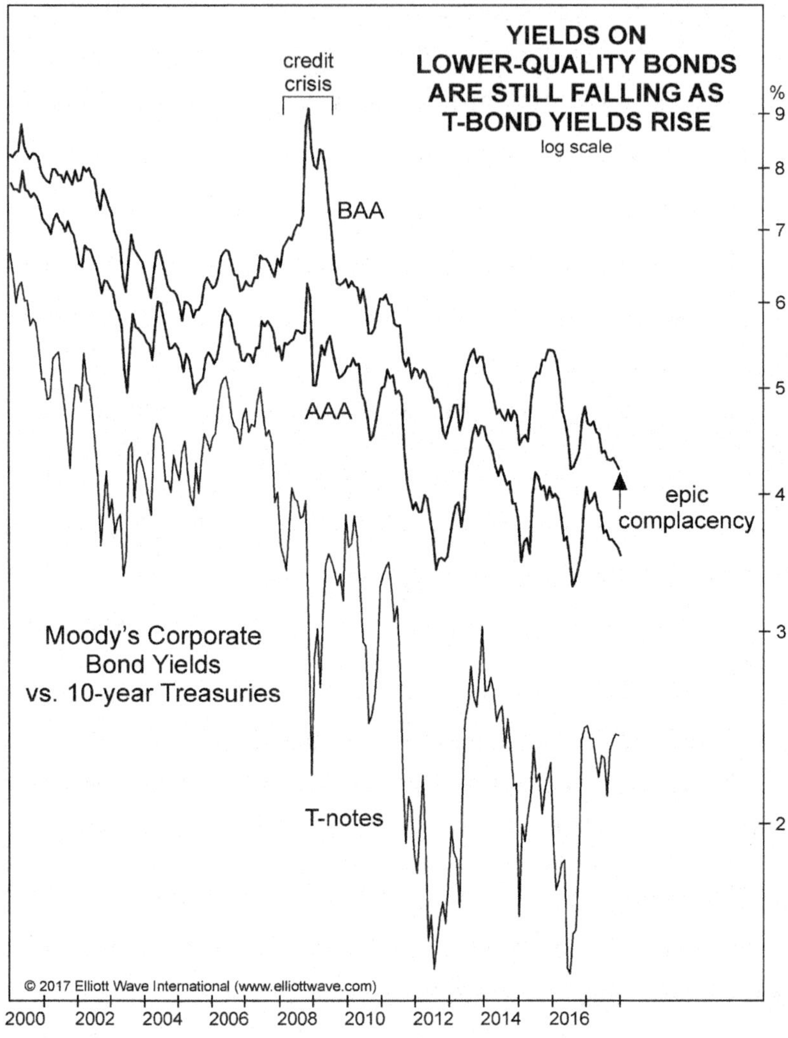

Figure 12-5

Bond prices finally bottomed in June 1932, stocks bottomed in July, and the economy bottomed in the first quarter of 1933. A half century later, bond prices bottomed in October 1981, stock prices bottomed in August 1982, and a recession ended in November 1982. If the same sequence occurs in the next major bottoming process, bond prices will bottom first, stock prices will bottom next, and the economy will hit bottom several months later.

Investor psychology should work like this: As social mood becomes less positive, investors will look for a haven buy bonds that they perceive to be safe. But as mood continues to trend toward the negative, fear will increase, deflation will accelerate, the incomes of businesses and governments will decline, and bond investors will begin to worry about losing their principal due to bankruptcy and default by bond issuers. That's when they will start selling bonds, making interest rates accelerate higher. Rates on the weakest issues will rise the fastest, but eventually fear will spread to holders even of formerly presumed safe paper. Finally, the economy will contract so severely that it reaches depression, forcing sales of good debt while wiping out weak debtors and therefore their creditors as well.

T-bonds enjoyed their longest and biggest bull market on record from 1981 to 2016. We at Elliott Wave International were able to recognize the peak in T-bond prices (low in yield) of July 2016 a week before it occurred. Although we believe that a bear market in bond prices is underway, low-grade bond yields have not even begun to climb. As shown in Figure 12-5, the premium on yields for BAA paper over yields for AAA paper has been narrowing for a year and a half. In line with continued predictions for a sustained economic recovery, bond buyers in 2017 remain in a state of epic complacency in the belief that lower-grade bonds are safe.

If rates on low-grade bonds begin rising as expected, some observers will probably be fooled. Bulls on the economy may take the new trend as a sign of economic expansion. Those betting on hyperinflation may take it as a sign that inflation is ready to soar. But the real reason for the rise in rates will be that investors will be exercising new-found caution by demanding higher rates due to fears of default.

Fears of default will not be misplaced. With a turn of Grand Supercycle degree approaching, the unfolding depression will be deeper than that of the early 1930s. Most debtors around the world *will* default.

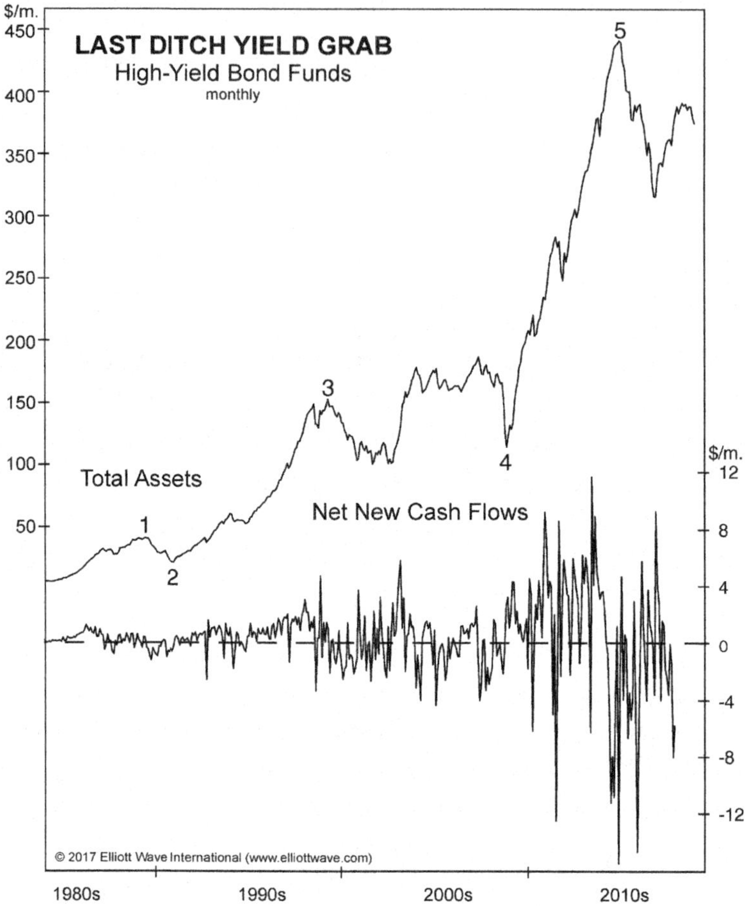

Figure 12-6

The Coming Yield-Spread Explosion

The recent spike to a lower high in high-yield mutual fund inflows (Figure 12-6) shows that investors have probably maxed out their reach for yield. Ownership of junk bonds funds is below the all-time high but still heavy. The impending downturn in junk bond prices will be bigger than any of the declines over the last 30 years. In the not-too-distant future, junk will finally live up to its name.

Today's "High-Grade" Bonds

Don't think that you will be safe buying bonds rated BBB or above. The unprecedented mass of vulnerable bonds extant today is on the verge of a waterfall of downgrading. Many bonds that are currently rated investment grade will be downgraded to junk status and then go into default. The downgrades will lag falling prices, so you will not be afforded advance warning of loss. When the big slide begins, I doubt that the rating services will even be able to keep up with the downgrades at the rate that they will be required.

One problem with owning government bonds is the political risk. Governments have a long record of stiffing their creditors in a crisis, as Puerto Rico recently did. No government is immune from adopting that solution to its financial problems. A new regime especially may have little regard for previously squandered credit.

Today, millions of individuals and institutions own tax-exempt municipal bonds. While there are assuredly many exceptions, this class of bonds is the riskiest among popular government issues. In the United States, default could happen to municipal bonds quite soon after times get difficult. Politicians in many jurisdictions have borrowed and spent way more money than is likely ever to be paid back. Merely paying the interest on that debt in tough economic times will become an acute problem for many issuers. In such cases, default for many cities and counties will be inevitable. Even the debt of some federal government agencies is at serious risk of default in a worst-case scenario.

The Answer to Bond Selection

So, if conventional wisdom is wrong, what is the correct way to frame the problem of investment opportunity and risk with respect to bonds in a deflationary depression? It is this: Any bond that is AAA at the start of the depression *and remains AAA throughout it* will be a satisfactory investment. The problem is, who can figure out which bonds those are? As we will see in Chapter 21, you cannot rely on bond rating services to guide you in a crunch.

If a crash and depression take place, some corporations whose products or services are important in that environment will become special situations, and their bonds will shine as viable investments. Unfortunately, I don't have the expertise to pick out the handful of long-term corporate bonds that will hold their value in a deflationary crash; I have only speculated on what will be some of the worst. In a deflationary depression, the biggest fools will be complacent creditors. They will get what they deserve. Don't be one of them.

Chapter 13:

Should You Invest in Real Estate?

The worst thing about real estate is its *lack of liquidity* during a bear market. At least in the stock market, when your shares are down 60% and you realize you've made a horrendous mistake, you can swiftly *get out* (unless you run a mutual fund, pension fund, insurance company or other institution with millions of shares, in which case, you're stuck). With real estate, you can't pick up the phone and sell. You need to find a *buyer* for your house in order to sell it. In a depression, buyers just go away. Mom and Pop move in with the kids, or the kids move in with Mom and Pop. People start living in their offices or moving their offices into their living quarters. Businesses close down. In time, there is a massive glut of real estate.

In the initial stages of a depression, sellers remain under an illusion about what their property is worth. They keep a high list price on their house, reflecting what it was worth at the peak. This stubbornness leads to a drop in sales volume. At some point, a few owners cave in and sell at much lower prices. Then others are forced to drop their prices, too. What is the potential *buyer's* psychology at that point? "Well, gee, property prices have been coming down. Why should I rush? I'll wait till they come down further." The further they come down, the more the buyer wants to wait. It's a downward spiral.

When Real Estate Falls

Real estate prices have always fallen hard when stock prices have fallen hard. Figure 13-1 displays this reliable relationship.

The overwhelming evidence for a major stock market decline is enough by itself to portend a tumble in real estate prices. Usually the culprit behind these joint declines is a credit deflation. If there were ever a time we were poised for such a decline, it is now.

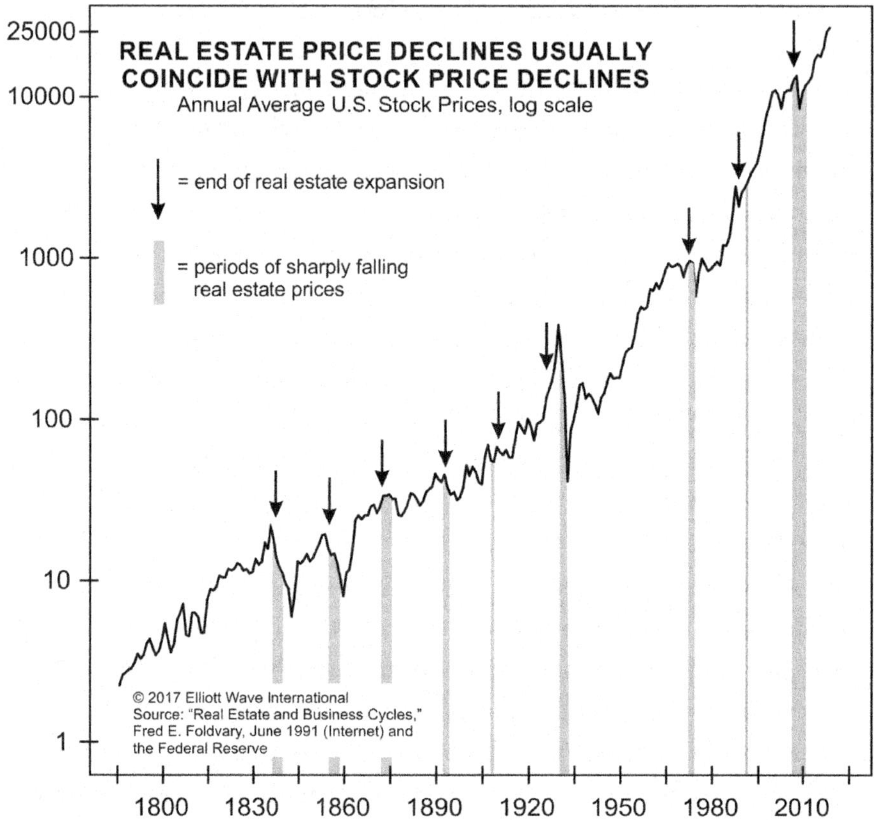

Figure 13-1

The Extension of Credit

What screams "bubble" — giant, historic bubble — in real estate today is the system-wide extension of *massive* amounts of credit to finance property purchases. As a result, a record percentage of Americans today are nominal "homeowners" via $10.6 trillion in mortgage debt. Seventy percent of them owe an average of 68% of the value of their homes, plus interest, and both ratios have been increasing.

People can buy a house with little or no down payment in many cases. They can refinance a house for its entire value. "How can this be?" you ask. "Isn't at least 20% homeowner equity required?" Well, sort of. Credit institutions are supposed to be penalized for lending more than 80% on an uninsured mortgage. But if they get it insured, which is generally not difficult, the limit can go up to 90%. With VA or FHA approval, it can go up to 95%. "Prime borrowers" can refinance for up to 125% of a home's appraised value.

The problem with low down payments is that their success and continuation depend upon continuously rising property prices. Once a bank extends a loan for most of a property's value, it essentially owns the house at that value. *Then, any drop in that value below that level causes a drop in the value of the bank's capital.* By contrast, when the bank lends only half of the value of a home, its value can drop as much as half, and the bank can still get all of its depositors' money out of the deal by selling the house.

Bank loans to home buyers are bad enough, but government-sponsored mortgage lenders — the Federal National Mortgage Corp. (Fannie Mae), the Federal Home Loan Mortgage Corp. (Freddie Mac) and the Federal Home Loan Banks — have extended $5 *trillion* worth of mortgage credit. Major financial institutions actually *invest* in huge packages of these mortgages, an investment that they and their clients (which may include you) will surely regret. In December 2001, Fannie Mae was the most widely held among institutions' favorite stocks. The first edition of *Conquer the Crash* cited *Money* magazine's report that the CEO of Fannie Mae "may be the most confident CEO in America." The book warned,

> Certainly his stockholders, clients and mortgage-package investors had better share that feeling, because confidence is the only

thing holding up this giant house of cards. When real estate prices begin to fall in a deflationary crash, lenders will experience a rising number of defaults on the mortgages they hold.

Confidence was indeed the only thing holding up the enterprise. Starting in 2002, the scheme collapsed, and so did Fannie Mae's stock price, as you can see in Figure 13-2.

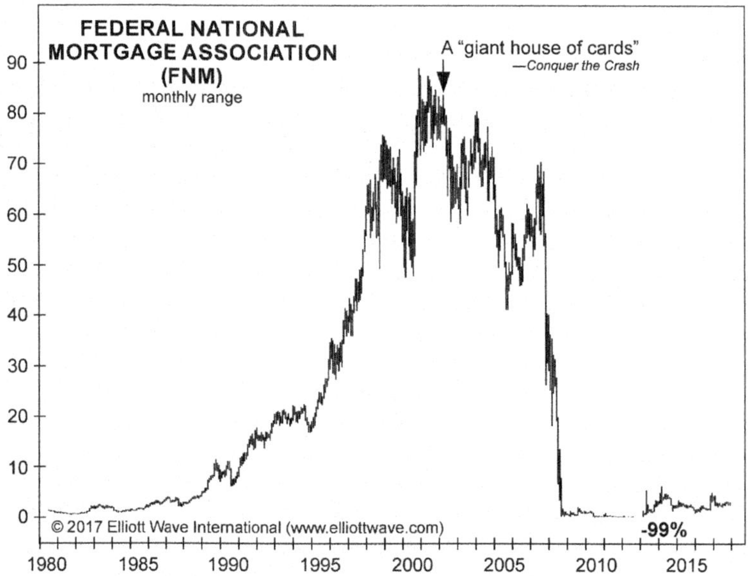

Figure 13-2

Another remarkable trend of recent years adds to the precarious nature of mortgage debt. Many people have been rushing to borrow the last pennies possible on their homes. They have been taking out home equity loans so they can buy stocks, TVs, vacations, cars, bitcoins, home remodeling services and whatever else their hearts desire at the moment. This widespread practice is brewing a *terrible* disaster. Taking out a home equity loan is nothing but turning ownership of your home over to your bank in exchange for whatever other items you would like to own or consume. It's a reckless course, and it stems from the extreme confidence — on both sides of these transactions — that accompanies a positive extreme in social mood.

At the bottom of the coming depression, banks are going to own many, many homes, and their previous owners will be out in the street. That's not so bad; at least they got their money's worth from the TVs and cars. It will be a disaster for the banks' depositors, though, because there will be no one to buy the homes at mortgage-value prices. Depositors' money will be stuck in lifeless property deals, marked down 50%, 90% or (as happened in the Great Depression) even more.

Real estate matters more than any other market, because bank deposits are backed by mortgages. When mortgages collapse in value, banks' assets will evaporate.

Credit expansion has supported real estate prices, but now it is late in the game. The low interest rates of recent years have spurred property sales, because financing rates appeared low. Marginal buyers, who had waited on the sidelines, finally took the plunge. People around the country think that now is their last great opportunity to buy property. Naturally, it is the opposite: It's your last chance to sell. The market is becoming as bought up as it can get, and there is no interest-rate ammunition left to win the battle for even more borrowers. Now the debt incurred by real estate buyers is a ball and chain around the market's neck. When the depression hits, even the seemingly attractive 3.5% mortgage will be tough to pay.

Although real estate prices have returned to their all-time highs, the recovery has been thin, as housing stocks have slackened and transaction volume is down, as you can see in Figures 13-3, 13-4 and 13-5.

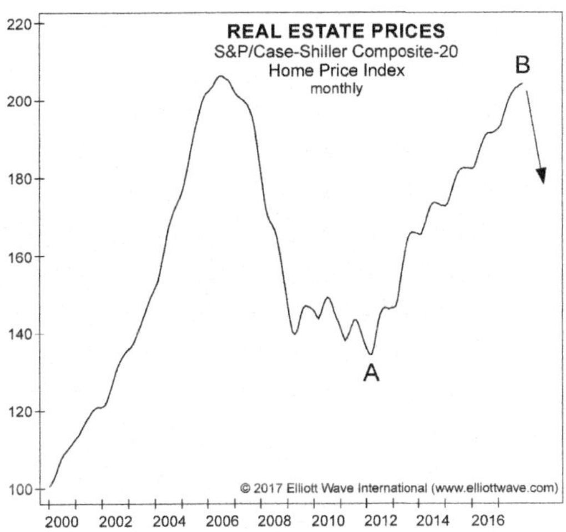

Figure 13-3

Figure 13-4

Figure 13-5

Underlying weakness in a recovery is characteristic of a bear market rally, or "B" wave. The Elliott wave labels in Figure 13-3 indicate that a bear market for real estate began in 2006. The implied C wave forecasts another wave of falling prices dead ahead.

Real estate investors, then, are in for a big surprise. The next wave down in real estate prices is likely to be even deeper and more prolonged than that of 2006-2012. When the institutional investors who bought properties in bulk finally give up on their holdings, there will be a glut of homes on the market, which will contribute to the price decline. In a few years, much of the newest batch of mortgage debt will become worthless.

This book is U.S.-centric, but the most vulnerable countries for a real estate debacle are Canada and China. Canadian real estate barely paused as U.S. prices fell in 2006-2012, and they zoomed to record heights into 2017, when people waited in lines to bid on a house. The Chinese government has funded massive overbuilding for years, even to the point of creating ghost cities. These trends are unsustainable and will reverse.

Some Things To Do

To avoid the property bust, you can take the following steps:

- Avoid investing in real estate investment trusts, which are perhaps the worst property-related investments during a bear market. Some REITs valued at $100 a share in the early 1970s fell to ¼ or ⅛ by late 1974, and most of them never recovered. REITs are sold to the public because the people who do the deals don't want to stick with them. The public falls for REITs cycle after cycle. These "investments" hold up in the best part of bull markets, but they are disasters in bear markets.

- Wrap up any real-estate sales you are working and get out of all investment real estate holdings that are not special situations about which you know much more than the market. In general, wait for lower prices to re-invest.

- If you hold a big mortgage on expensive property that depends upon public patronage, such as an arena, playhouse, amusement park, arts center or other such facility, consider selling it or subleasing it insured.

- If you are a banker, sell off your largest-percentage mortgages and get into safer investments.

- If you rent your living or office space, try to arrange it so that your lease either allows you to leave on short notice or has a clause lowering your rent if like units are reduced in price.

- If you have a huge mortgage on a McMansion or condo that you cannot afford unless your current income maintains, sell it and move into something more reasonable. If at all possible, join the 34% of title-holding Americans who own their homes outright. Be willing to trade down to make it happen. See Chapter 23 for more on this topic.

- If you consider your home a consumption item, and you wish to keep it on that basis, fine. But if you are just as happy renting a residence as owning, do so.

- At the bottom, buy the home, office building or business facility of your dreams for ten cents or less per dollar of its peak value.

Chapter 14:

Should You Invest in Collectibles?

Collecting for Investment

Collecting for investment purposes is almost always foolish. First of all, never buy anything *marketed* as a collectible. It breaks my heart to see *USA Today* and our local paper run full-page ads for virtually worthless junk coins and bars of base metals, carefully written and photographed to manipulate the ignorant and gullible into thinking they are making a sound investment while technically avoiding making deceptive statements. Even in honest transactions, the chances of losing money when collectibility is priced into an item are huge. Most collecting trends are fads. They might be short-run or long-run fads, but they eventually dissolve. The inflation of the 1970s pushed gold and silver higher, so rare coins got a free ride of new interest. What did coin rarity have to do with inflation? Nothing.

Except perhaps for certain enduring masters' works, the focus of art appreciation goes through cycles. So do prices, even for the best art.

There are times when collecting makes sense, but you have to be in on the ground floor. When I was a kid, I collected coins at a time when you could find rare coins in everyday pocket change. In the 1950s, my grandmother persuaded the town council to let her sort through the weekly take of coins from parking meters and exchange them one for one. There was *no downside* to the hobby because the coins were always worth at least face value.

In depressions, people care about gold or silver content in coins, not rarity. One company that specializes in liquidating U.S. coin collections is American Federal, which can broker your coins or buy them outright. Be sure to compare prices with other dealers, some of which are listed in Chapter 19. Here is the contact information:

American Federal Rare Coin & Bullion
President: Nick Grovich
Website: americanfederal.com
Email: info@americanfederal.com
Address: P.O. Box 5810
Carefree, AZ 85377-5810
Phone: 1-800-221-7694 or 480-553-5282
Fax: 480-553-5290

Also taking a hard-nosed, consumer-advocacy stance is the *Rosen Numismatic Advisory*, which has won many awards over its 27 years of publication. If you prefer handling your own financial dealings, this is a good source of buy-and-sell coin strategies, information and advice. Here's how to get in touch:

Rosen Numismatic Advisory
President: Maurice Rosen
Numismatic Counseling, Inc.
Email: mauricerosen@aol.com
Address: PO Box 38
Plainview, NY 11803
Phone: 516-433-5800
Fax: 516-433-5801

Many collectibles, including coins and stamps, have already retreated from their all-time highs. Yet baseball cards and comic books still have significant value. Rock 'n' roll memorabilia and other baby-boomer collectibles are probably at an all-time top.

Baby boomers who covet reminders of their youth will die off in the next 30 years, and most of their collectibles will be considered little more than curios.

If you want to sell your everyday collectibles, few venues are better than eBay. For fine art sales, contact:

Christie's
Website: christies.com
Address: 20 Rockefeller Place
New York, NY 10020
Phone: 212-646-2000
Fax: 212-636-2399

Sotheby's
Website: sothebys.com
Address: 1334 York Ave
New York, NY 10021
Phone: 212-606-7000/541-312-5682
Fax: 212-606-7107/541-312-5684

Collecting for Pleasure

If you collect certain items for the love of them, you are about to be made very happy. Prices for art and collectibles will fall to joyously affordable levels in a depression. If you want to enhance your collection, keep your capital safe, wait until the bottom, and buy up all the items you want at pennies on today's dollar value.

Chapter 15:

Should You Invest in "Cash"?

Today's Precarious Conditions

Today, we're in a situation far more precarious than that of 1929. People have gorged on investments. They own debt in the forms of junk bonds, muni bonds, corporates and mortgages. They are invested in real estate and expecting a boom. They own stocks at record prices under the belief that a "Trump bull market" is just getting going. They own precious metals, which are stagnant. And they've got bank accounts, which are IOUs backed by IOUs. There is a widespread, unstated conviction that you have to *own something*, that whatever you do, *don't hold cash*, because cash is trash.

Tell that to the people who live in Cyprus. When access to credit was curtailed in 2013, there was a soaring demand for cash — the one thing nobody had. A March 26, 2013 article in *The Financial Times* reported, "The most immediate problem confronting businesses was a scarcity of cash." A businessman in Cyprus said, "The market is operating on a cash basis—everybody wants cash." That was the immediate result of deflation in Cyprus. When you look at the sea of large mortgages on which most bank deposits depend, it is not hard to imagine something similar happening in the United States and around the world.

The Wonder of Cash

Financial advisors' battle cry is "diversification." They recommend having your assets spread out in numerous different *stocks*, numerous different stock *funds*, numerous different "emerging" foreign stock *markets*, an array of properties, high-yield bonds, muni bonds and/or a slew of "alternative investments" such as commodities. Advocates of junk bonds likewise counsel prospective investors that having lots of different issues will reduce risk.

This "strategy" is bogus. Why invest in anything unless you have a strong opinion about where it's going and a game plan for when to get out? Diversification is gospel today, because investment assets of so many kinds have gone up for so long, but the future is another matter. Owning an array of investments is financial *suicide* during deflation. They all go down, and the logistics of getting out of them can be a nightmare. Aside from weird exceptions, such as gold in the early 1930s, when the government fixed the price, or perhaps some commodity that is crucial in a war, *all assets go down in price during deflation except one: cash.*

Today, few people give cash a thought. Because interest rates are "too low," investors claim that they have "no choice" but to invest in something with "upside potential." Ironically but obviously necessarily, the last major interest-rate cycle was perfectly aligned to convince people to do the wrong thing. In the early 1980s, when rates were high, people thought that stocks were not worth buying. Now that rates are low, they think that cash is not worth holding. It's a psychological trap keeping investors from doing the right thing: buying stocks at the bottom (when rates were high) and selling them at the top (when rates are low).

Now let's dispose of the idea that the return on cash is always "low." How would you like to own a safe asset that goes up over five times in value in nineteen years? Figure 15-1 is a picture of the soaring value of cash in Japan from 1990 through 2008. Cash appreciated over 400% in terms of how many shares of Japanese stocks it could buy. Figure 15-2 is one picture of the rising value of cash in the United States, which appreciated 287 percent from

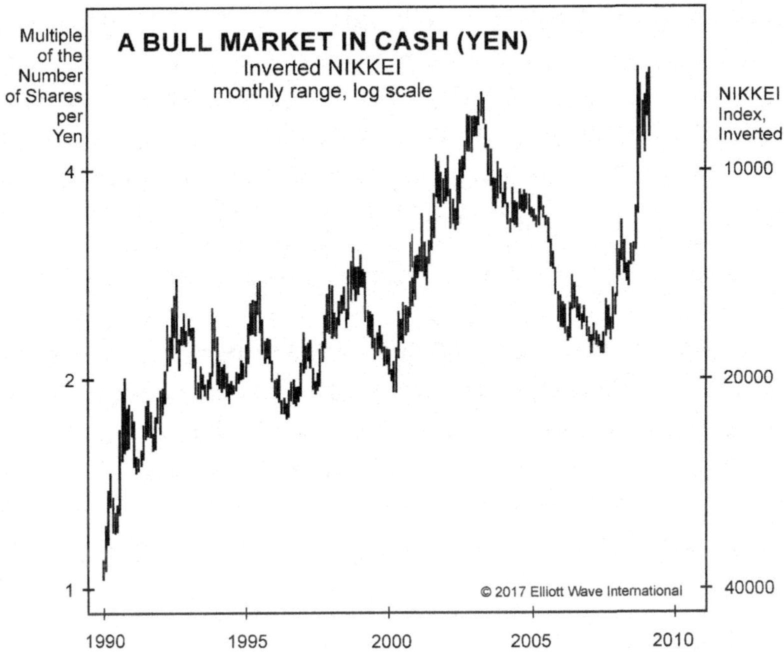

Figure 15-1

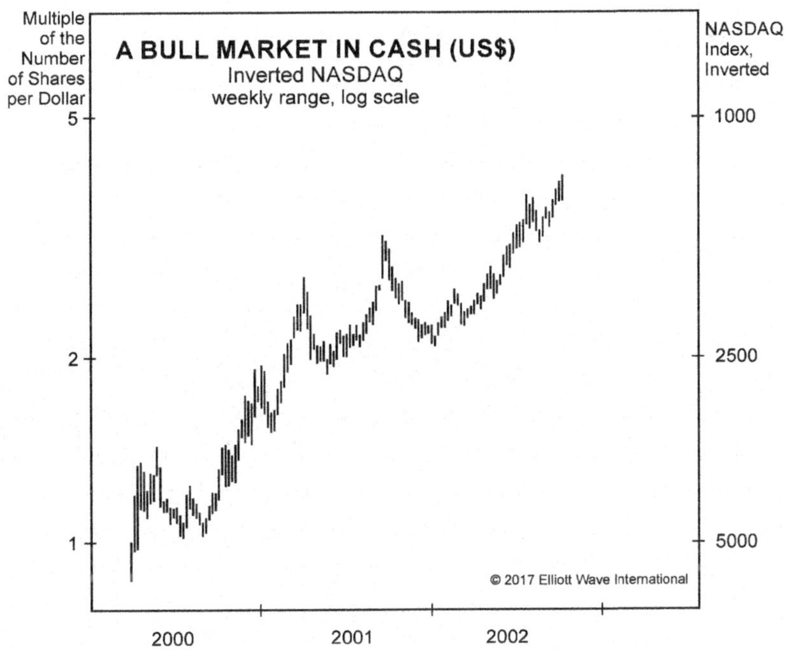

Figure 15-2

March 2000 to October 2002 in terms of how many shares of the NASDAQ index it could buy. Wouldn't you like to enjoy this kind of performance, too? You can, if you move into cash before a major deflation. Then when the stock market reaches bottom, you can buy incredibly cheap shares that almost no one else can afford because they lost it all when their stocks collapsed.

Cash is the only asset that assuredly rises in value during deflation. One safe "parking place" for capital during a deflationary crash is cash notes — for example, $100 bills, £50 notes or the equivalent in your home currency — in a safe depository to which you will always have access. That way, you will have money if the bank fails, you will have money if credit collapses, and you will have money if the government defaults on its debt. I suggest that you have at least *some* currency on hand to buy gas and groceries if you expect a deflationary crash.

Unfortunately, currency has no yield, it is destructible, and it cannot be transferred with a phone call. Carefully selected "cash equivalents" can solve those problems for larger amounts of money.

The Risk in Many "Cash Equivalents"

Cash equivalents are high-quality short-term debt. They are extremely attractive investments in a deflationary crash. Choosing them, however, can be tricky. You must own *safe* instruments held at a *safe* facility.

Most cautious investors think that their funds are safe, even guaranteed, in any money market fund. Do not fall for this illusion. Money market funds are *relatively* safe, but they are still nothing but portfolios of debt, short-term debt to be sure, but debt nonetheless. When a company or government goes bankrupt, it stops paying interest on its debts, short-term or long, *right then*. If you own any of it at the time, your investment is compromised, if not gone.

In a strong economy, few give this risk any thought. They do not imagine that companies, governments and their agencies will ever cease paying interest due. Many people also erroneously believe that the debt issued by government-sponsored enterprises are government-guaranteed, but they're not. Ultimately, *you* take the risk when you buy their debt or their investment products.

Some money market funds realized early on that they could buy slightly riskier debt issues in order to squeeze out an extra 0.1% annual yield above that of their competitors, which they could then advertise to attract deposits. Others began to try to top *them* using the same tactics. Some funds have ended up owning a lot of weak debt. To the extent that a money-market fund's holdings are downgraded, the fund is that much riskier. Funds do not report downgrades to you or warn you if they think any of their holdings may be at risk. You hear about it only when it has to explain to you the loss statement that you receive in the mail.

In a depression, many money market funds will shock their depositors when they report losses. Once the process of debt defaults begins, to whom — and at what price — will the funds sell their portfolios if they wish to replace their risky assets with safer ones? They are all on the same ship, and there are few lifeboats.

The Safest Cash Equivalents Inside the U.S.

The safest cash equivalents in a depression are the very best near-term debt instruments, issued by a strong enterprise or government. In the U.S., the primary option is short-term Treasury securities, a category that includes not only Treasury bills but also longer-term notes and bonds that are within months of maturity, which can be purchased on the secondary market. For the time being, and for the investor who must or prefers to keep all assets inside the United States, Treasury bills or money market funds that hold only short-term U.S. Treasury debt appear to be the best financial haven available next to bullion-type gold and silver coins. The best way to own T-bills is through a safe bank. (See Chapter 16.)

In 1980-1982, T-bills were #1 on investors' buy list, and that's just when they should have held zero T-bills, because in fact it was time to own stocks and bonds. Now stocks and bonds are tops on investors' buy list, but they should be holding zero stocks and bonds, because it's time to own cash and safe cash equivalents.

The beauty of safe, near-term debt is that instead of getting killed by rising interest rates, you can benefit from them. In 1931, the Fed raised its discount rate in the face of deflation in order to prop up the value of a falling dollar. Other investments fell harder as a result, but holders of very short-term T-bills who kept purchasing new ones at expiration watched their returns increase. This is a good way to defend your portfolio against rising interest rates.

A Treasury bill or Treasury-only money market fund has the added advantage of incurring no state income tax obligation on the interest it pays, which saves you some money if you live in a state with an income tax. You can also write checks on a money-market account, so you will be getting a fairly safe yield on what amounts to your checking account. Usually individual check amounts must be $100 or more, so you will still need a bank account for smaller checks, but that shouldn't put much of your total wealth at risk. Many money-market funds are bonded by insurance companies against fraud or theft, but in a depression environment, such a bond is only as good as its insurer (see Chapter 20). Also, if the fund's custodial bank fails, your T-bills could be under wraps until things are sorted out.

You could choose to buy Treasury bills directly from a broker or the U.S. Treasury Department from instructions available at its websites at www.publicdebt.treas.gov. and www.treasurydirect.gov. For the record, you no longer get actual Treasury bills for your money. You get a bookkeeping entry that *says* you own Treasury bills. The Treasury department makes it easy to roll over your position automatically upon expiration, but on the other hand, you get none of the amenities of a money-market fund. Subscribers, moreover, have complained to me of the unweildiness of the Treasury's website, and who knows if it will operate properly in an environment of monetary chaos? So, there are some risks even in owning T-bills, whether directly or indirectly.

Of the many hundreds of money market funds in the United States, surprisingly few hold exclusively short-term U.S. Treasury obligations. Among the largest fifteen of these funds, only three — as listed in Table 15-1 — have all these features: no other required accounts, no transaction limits, and no separate charges for printing checks, bounced checks or wire transfers into or out of your account. All of these funds' costs are covered by their "expense ratios," i.e., the percentage of your account that they charge as a management fee.

New York Mellon Bank owns Dreyfus, which could prove problematic. American Century is independent. Vanguard has very low fees for large accounts and a low expense ratio. Unfortunately, all these funds retain the privilege of restricting outflows at their discretion, which is a scary prospect. Fund policies change over time, so be sure that you completely understand a fund's investment strategy and prospectus before committing any money.

STILL-AVAILABLE TREASURY-ONLY MONEY MARKET FUNDS WITH NO TRANSACTION CHARGES OR LIMITS		
Fund Name	**Toll-Free No.**	**Web Address**
American Century Capital Presv Fund I	(800) 345-2021	www.americancentury.com
Dreyfus 100% US Treasury MMF	(800) 782-6620	www.dreyfus.com
Vanguard Federal Money Market Fund	(877) 662-7447	www.vanguard.com

Table 15-1

A Most Convenient Alternative

Among all options, perhaps the best idea is to invest in something the government has only recently begun offering: 2-year U.S. Floating Rate Notes (FRNs). The interest rate paid on FRNs is pegged to the 13-week T-bill and adjusts quarterly to the auction rate. You can learn more about FRNs by going to the Treasury's website at www.TreasuryDirect.gov and typing "FRN" into the search window.

With short rates just coming off zero, the lowest level ever, there seems little chance of losing principal in an FRN. U.S. rates have never fallen below zero, and even if inflation rages—contrary to my expectations—rates should rise to compensate. That's a lot to like.

With FRNs, you avoid the hassle of rolling over T-bills every three months. More important, there will probably be a shortage of T-bills when the panic hits, just as there was a shortage of Swiss Money Market Claims in 2008. Investors were turned away, and their nearest option was Eurodollar debts, which were not nearly as safe. Owners of FRNs are safely locked in for the two-year duration of the notes.

If rates on federal debt rise, FRNs will keep paying out more and more despite deflation, making them extremely lucrative. Holders will be getting bigger and bigger payouts of increasingly valuable money.

Like any other Treasury security, you can buy or sell these notes in the open market, so you don't have to wait until the next auction to buy or until they mature to cash out. Also, interest earned is untaxable at the state and local level. Your safe bank can buy FRNs on your behalf, or you can buy them through Treasury Direct.

While I am comfortable saying that T-bills are the safest asset to hold inside the United States this side of gold and silver, someday even Treasury bills would probably become risky. If the dollar re-enters its long term bear market, and particularly if it goes into free-fall, then even soaring short-term Treasury yields might be unable to overcome investors' imperative to get out. Each uptick in yield would be a yet greater burden to the government in the form of debt service, a fact that might frighten T-bill investors as much as entice them.

The only way for holders of Treasury bills and FRNs to lose all their money would be for the U.S. government to default on its debt. A federal government default is not impossible. The U.S. Treasury's $21 trillion debt and extensive unfunded liabilities will present significant financial burdens in a depression. The deepest depression in three centuries could force Treasury issues down to junk status, like so many South American IOUs. If the federal government defaults, it might resort to a desperate action such as declaring that Treasury bills are now long-term bonds, to be paid off in thirteen years instead of thirteen weeks. You don't want to be stuck with any such deal.

Despite this risk, the U.S. government still has immense taxing power, and its world-class reputation should attract a share of capital if there is a "flight to quality" during a worldwide monetary crisis. As many stocks and bonds collapse during the crash, those who thought they were pretty smart for investing in historically overpriced stocks, overpriced bonds, retail consumer debt and worse will come to realize, "We need to sell these losers for what we can get and buy something safe with the money we have left." In such a situation, money is likely to flow into what investors perceive as stronger issues. They are likely to include Treasury bills, making their issuer, the U.S. Treasury, even more liquid. Of course, politics could scuttle this potential. Foreign governments could outlaw money exports, or the U.S. could become politically unstable, reducing its status as an investment haven. The truth is that no one can know exactly how Treasury securities will fare in a major depression. What I *can* say is that, apart from special situations in the corporate realm that I dare not attempt to identify, T-bills and FRNs are probably the safest U.S.-based interest-bearing investments.

If you ever come to believe that T-bills will get into trouble, you should buy safe foreign short-term debt or gold and silver to protect your capital. For details, see the next section and

Chapter 19. Always be vigilant; always be practical; always try to get out of a potentially risky investment *before* others perceive that risk. If you need help anticipating such changes, Elliott Wave International continuously monitors these markets from the standpoint of price trends and investor psychology.

Finding the Safest Cash Equivalents Outside the U.S.

For the globally sophisticated investor, there are excellent alternatives to U.S.-based debt. Most people hesitate to look outside their own areas, but if you have substantial capital to protect, you should expand your geographical horizons. The first reason is for the sake of diversity (*targeted* diversity, not the willy-nilly type), but there is a better reason: The safest investment debt resides within the safest financial systems. The strongest cash equivalents today lie *outside* the United States.

Even if a debt-issuing *entity* is financially secure, events that are barely its fault might compromise it. For example, a manufacturer or municipality might be fully sound, except that it unwarily entrusts all its accounts to a single bank, and the bank fails. Suddenly, the issuing entity is in financial trouble, and its debt is much riskier.

So, ideally, you should begin by identifying a country whose financial system is among the soundest available. According to SafeWealth Group and GNS Hillier Capital, two firms of wealth preservation experts, Switzerland is the standout in this respect in Europe, and Singapore is the standout in Asia, currently and for the immediately foreseeable future.

Swiss voters are — relatively speaking — financially conservative. Under the Swiss Constitution, citizen-led referendums and initiatives can, and often do, challenge or revoke bad government policies or legislation, keeping excesses in check. Swiss citizens also have the highest savings rate in Europe, which helps keep the local banking system liquid. Singapore issues little short-term debt because the government, with its conservative spending policy, doesn't need much short-term money. The country's bank reserves are strong because its citizens have a 25% savings rate mandated by law, which they routinely exceed. For comparison, the savings rate in the U.S. has been hovering near 2.5%. Moreover, each of these countries has a relatively small total government debt relative to its financial base. Switzerland's national debt is only about 200 billion Swiss francs, a fraction of the 1.77 trillion Sfr deposited in that country's banks, much of which would surely be available to refinance Swiss government debt given difficult times, when capital seeks conservative investments. Thus, while keeping in mind that politics can change, it appears at this time far less likely that a Swiss or Singaporean government entity will renege on its jurisdiction's obligations than perhaps any other government entities in the world.

The next step is to find the safest debt issues within one or both of the safest countries. In Switzerland, Swiss Money Market Claims (the equivalent of T-bills), near-term Swiss Confederation bonds and carefully selected cantonal (a canton is a state) bonds are probably as close to safe debt as you can get. Singapore's safest offerings are long-term government bonds with nearby maturities.

To be even safer, you will want to get more specific. While most Swiss cantons' paper has a top safety rating, the standard rating services, as we will see in Chapter 21, do not take the possibility of severe system-wide financial pressures into account. It is advisable, then, to invest in cantons that have little debt and whose bonds have a modicum of liquidity.

As you can probably tell by now, this is a field for specialists. I am not one of them. If you are a major institution or Arab oil magnate, you may already get good advice. But otherwise, as far as I know, the SafeWealth Group and Hillier Capital are the best options. SafeWealth has researched banks globally, ranked them for liquidity and safety and forged relationships with the best of them. Hillier is a safety-minded money manager whose focus is on safety, liquidity and geographical diversification. Hillier is aware of EWI's list of stable currencies and recommended jurisdictions, and it prefers holding assets in the handful of countries that have smaller governments, big markets, high savings rates and liquid banking systems. Wherever you reside, if you would like to own a portfolio of the safest short-term foreign debt or even a fund of U.S. Treasury bills through a safe Swiss or Singaporean institution, these are a good places to start. Be aware that these companies require minimum investments, as cited below. You may contact them as follows:

GNS Hillier Capital
Address: 250 Monroe Avenue, Suite 400
Grand Rapids, Michigan 49423
Phone: 616-886-3022
Director: Michael Smorch
Email: michael@gnshillierpartners.com
Minimum: $2 million

SafeWealth Group Service Center
Cari Lima, Senior Vice President
Email: clientservices@safewealthgroup.ch
Address: CP 476, 1000 Lausanne, 30 Grey, Switzerland
Phone: (from U.S. 011) 41-21-641-1640
Fax: (from U.S. 011) 41-21-641-1640-1390
Minimum: $100,000

Equally comforting, these firms traditionally counsel people as if a global financial disaster lay immediately around the corner, so you don't have to explain concerns that most investment counselors view as little different from paranoia. As the old saying goes, I may be paranoid, but that doesn't mean there isn't someone following me. In the final analysis, it is better to be safe and wrong than exposed and wrong.

Protecting Against Hyperinflation

When a state follows the course of printing banknotes rapidly to fund its spending, the result is hyperinflation. I expect deflation in the U.S., not inflation. Nevertheless, I conceded in Chapter 10 that monetary foresight cannot be 20/20. Also, you may live in a country that is in a position to hyperinflate.

If you face a currency-based hyperinflation, some aspects of your financial defense are substantially different from those that you will use to protect against deflation. For example, you do not want to hold *anything* denominated in the hyperinflating currency, and you do not want to sell local stocks short. You can protect yourself best with a portfolio of notes and bills denominated in stable foreign currencies, along with gold and silver (see Chapter 19).

A Combination Strategy

Observe that one defense works for both a deflationary crash *and* a local hyperinflation: *holding notes and bills of strong issuers, denominated in a stable currency*. If you are worried about either deflation or hyperinflation in your country and want to protect against it, you should bank with an institution through which you can hold a portfolio of the highest-grade near-term debt with the option of switching its denomination easily from one currency to another so that you can keep your money continuously lodged with the most conservative and stable governments. Of course, if a worldwide hyperinflation were to spare no currency at all, then precious metals would be your primary recourse. To prepare even for that remote possibility, your bank should also be equipped to convert your holdings quickly to precious metals. If you can meet the minimum deposit requirements associated with their recommended institutions, SafeWealth Group can recommend a bank that will make all these arrangements under one roof. If your assets are below the required minimums, you can still achieve close to the desired result by choosing the most liquid banks, money market funds and precious metals available to you, using the lists and leads in this chapter and Chapters 16 and 19 as a guide. If you are among those with very low assets, carefully held cash and a minimal bank account should serve the goal of safety.

Chapter 16:

How To Find a Safe Bank

Risks in Banking

Between 1929 and 1933, 9000 banks in the United States closed their doors. President Roosevelt shut down *all* banks for a short time after his inauguration. In December 2001, the government of Argentina froze virtually all bank deposits, barring customers from withdrawing the money they thought they had. In 2013, banks in Cypress were ordered closed. Sometimes such restrictions happen naturally, when banks fail; sometimes they are imposed. Sometimes the restrictions are temporary; sometimes they remain in place for a long time.

In 2008-2009, some U.S. banks came under pressure of insolvency, just as the first edition of *Conquer the Crash* predicted. Fed bailouts kept most of them open. In the next depression, bank runs and mass closings are far more probable.

Conquer the Crash also noted that depositors would become concerned about bank risks and move their money from weak banks to strong banks, making the weak banks weaker and the strong banks stronger. This is just what happened in 2008-9. A *Washington Post* article noted that one of the banks listed in CTC as safer than most had received a windfall of migratory deposits. When the next wave of banking problems hits, the shift will be even more pronounced.

Why do banks fail? The word "deposit" as used by banks is borderline fraudulent in implying that the bank is holding your money for safekeeping. For 200 years, however, the courts have sanctioned an interpretation of the term "deposit" to mean *not* funds that you deliver for safekeeping but a *loan* to your bank. Your bank balance, then, is an IOU from the bank to you, payable on demand. Legally speaking, you have a claim on your money lent to a bank, but practically speaking, ultimately you have a claim only on the loans that the bank makes with your money. If a large portion of your bank's loans is tied up or becomes worthless, your money claim is compromised. A bank failure simply means that the bank has reneged on its promise to pay you back. The bottom line is that your money is only as safe as the bank's loans. In boom times, banks become imprudent and lend to almost anyone. In busts, they can't get much of that money back due to widespread defaults. If the bank's portfolio collapses in value, the bank is broke, and its depositors' savings are gone.

Because U.S. banks are no longer required to hold any of their deposits in reserve (see Chapter 6), many banks keep on hand just the bare minimum amount of cash needed for everyday transactions. Others keep a bit more. According to the latest Fed figures, the net loan-to-deposit ratio at U.S. commercial banks is 75.3 percent. This figure omits loans considered "securities" such as corporate, municipal and mortgage-backed bonds, which from my point of view are nearly as dangerous as everyday bank loans, although they are more liquid. Regardless, they are but more IOUs. The true loan-to-deposit ratio, then, is over 100 percent. Banks are not just lent to the hilt; they're past it. Some bank loans, at least in the current benign environment, could be liquidated quickly, but in a fearful market, liquidity even on debt "securities" will dry up. If just a few more depositors than normal were to withdraw money, banks would have to sell some of these assets, depressing prices and depleting the value of the securities remaining in their portfolios. If enough depositors were to attempt simultaneous withdrawals, banks would have to refuse. Banks with the lowest liquidity ratios will be particularly susceptible to runs in a depression.

You might think that banks would learn to behave differently with centuries of history to guide them, but for the most part, they haven't. The pressure to show good earnings to stockholders and to offer competitive interest rates to depositors induces them to make risky loans. The Federal Reserve's promise to be a last-resort lender has encouraged banks to lend aggressively, so far without deadly repercussion, although the experience of 2008 was something akin to a heart attack that the patient survived. Unfortunately, the patient is still gorging on artery-clogging foods. The U.S. government's Federal Deposit Insurance Corporation guarantees to refund depositors' losses up to $250,000, which *seems* to make safety a moot point. Actually, this guarantee just makes things worse, for two reasons. First, it removes a major motivation for banks to be conservative with your money. Depositors feel safe, so who cares what's going on behind closed doors? Second, did you know that most of the FDIC's money comes from other banks? This funding scheme makes prudent banks pay to save the imprudent ones, imparting weak banks' frailty to the strong ones. When the FDIC rescues weak banks by charging healthier ones higher "premiums," overall bank deposits are depleted, causing the net loan-to-deposit ratio to rise. This result, in turn, means that in times of bank stress, it will take a progressively smaller percentage of depositors demanding cash to cause unmanageable bank runs. If banks collapse in great enough quantity, the FDIC will be unable to rescue them all, and the more it charges surviving banks in "premiums," the more banks it will endanger. Thus, this form of insurance compromises the entire system. Ultimately, the federal government guarantees the FDIC's deposit insurance, which sounds like a sure thing. But if tax receipts fall, the government will be hard pressed to save a large number of banks with its own diminishing supply of capital. The FDIC calls its sticker "a symbol of confidence," and that's exactly what it is.

Some states in the U.S., in a fit of deadly "compassion," have made it illegal for a bank to seize the home of someone who has declared bankruptcy. In such situations, the bank and its depositors are on the hook indefinitely for borrowers' unthrift. Other states have made it illegal for a bank attempting to recover the value of a loan to seize any of a defaulting mortgage holder's assets other than the mortgaged property. In such situations, the bank assumes the price risk in the real estate market. These states' banks are vulnerable to severe losses in their mortgage portfolios and are at far greater risk of failure.

Many major national and international banks around the world have huge portfolios of "emerging market" debt, mortgage debt, consumer debt and weak corporate debt. I cannot understand how a bank trusted with the custody of your money could ever have even *thought* of buying bonds issued by Venezuela or Puerto Rico or any other unstable or spendthrift government. As I have put it, "Today's emerging markets will become *sub*merging markets." The fact that banks and other investment companies can repeatedly ride such "investments" all the way down to *write-offs* is outrageous.

Many banks today also have a shockingly large exposure to leveraged derivatives. The underlying value of assets represented by financial derivatives at quite a few big banks is greater than the total value of all their deposits. As noted earlier, the estimated representative value of all OTC derivatives in the world today is $542 trillion, about half of which is held by U.S. banks. Many banks use derivatives to hedge against investment exposure, but that strategy works only if the speculator on the other side of the trade can pay off if he's wrong.

Relying upon, or worse, speculating in, leveraged derivatives poses one of the greatest risks to banks that have succumbed to the lure. Leverage almost *always* causes massive losses eventually because of the psychological stress that owning them induces. It is traditional to discount the representative value of derivatives because traders will presumably get out of losing positions well before they cost as much as what they represent. Well, maybe. It is at least as common a human reaction for speculators to double their bets when the market goes against a big position. At least, that's what bankers might do with your money. You do not hear about this from bankers, because for bankers to educate depositors about investment safety would be to disturb their main source of profits.

Today's bank analysts assure us that banks are well capitalized. Unfortunately, that condition is mostly thanks to the great asset mania, which is probably ending. Much of the record amount of credit that banks have extended, such as that lent for productive enterprise or directly to strong governments, is relatively safe. Much of what has been lent to weak governments, real estate developers, government-sponsored enterprises, stock market speculators, venture capitalists, bitcoin investors, consumers, and so on, is not. One expert advised, "The larger, more diversified banks at this point are the safer place to be." That assertion will surely be severely tested in the coming depression. In my view, conservatively local run banks — a few of which exist — will prove to be safer.

There are five major conditions in place at many banks that pose a danger: (1) low liquidity levels, (2) dangerous exposure to leveraged derivatives, (3) the optimistic safety ratings of banks and their debt investments, (4) inflated values for the property that borrowers have put up as collateral on loans and (5) the substantial size of the mortgages that their clients hold compared both to the underlying property values and to the clients' potential inability to make payments under adverse circumstances. All of these conditions compound the risk to the banking system of deflation and depression.

Well before a worldwide depression dominates our daily lives, you will need to deposit your capital into safe institutions. I suggest using at least two to spread the risk. They must be far better than the ones that today are too optimistically deemed "liquid" and "safe" by rating services and banking officials.

Safe Banking in the United States

If you must bank in the U.S., or if you prefer it, choose the best bank(s) available. I believe that even in a deflationary crash, many of the safest U.S. banks have a good shot at survival and even prosperity. The reason is that relatively safe banks, if they have the sense to inform the public of their safety advantage, are likely to become *even safer* during difficult times. As noted earlier, depositors in a developing financial crisis will move funds out of the weakest banks into the strongest ones, making the weak ones weaker and the strong ones stronger. One of the great ironies of banking is that the more liquid a bank, the less likely it is that depositors will conduct a run on it in the first place.

There are a few independent and reliable bank rating sources. Among them, Veribanc, Inc. has been in the ratings business the longest. The service covers banks, S&Ls and credit unions. The company's classifications rank financial institutions not just on their present standing but also on their future outlook, which is what you should care about. Using a clear, simple rating system, it assesses capital strength, asset quality, management ability, earnings sufficiency, liquidity and sensitivity to market risk.

Weiss Ratings and IDC Financial Publishing, Inc. also publish specific and easy-to-interpret quarterly financial ratings that track the financial safety of U.S.-based banks, savings and loan institutions and credit unions. You will find contact information for these firms below:

IDC Financial Publishing, Inc.
Website: www.idcfp.com
Email: info@idcfp.com
Address: P.O. Box 140
Hartland, WI 53029
Phone: 800-525-5457 and 262-367-7231
Fax: 262-367-6497

Veribanc, Inc.
Website: www.veribanc.com
Email: service@veribanc.com
Address: P.O. Box 608
Greenville, RI 02828
Phone: 800-837-4226
Fax: 401-531-2290

Weiss Ratings, LLC
Website: www.weissratings.com
Address: 15430 Endeavour Dr.
Jupiter FL 33478
Phone: 877-934-7778
Fax: 561-277-2576

Observe that the biggest, best-known and most widely followed rating services, which had long been sanctioned by government regulators, are *not* on my list and were not on my list in the original edition of this book. That proved to be a wise decision, as the ratings posted by those firms blew up in 2008-2009, crushing the finances of the people who relied on them. Generally speaking, it pays to deal with independent judges who have no obligation to those whom they judge and no special privileges or designations granted by government.

Do not assume that once you find a relatively safe bank you can simply move all of your funds to it and sleep soundly. Bank ratings can change. The smart approach is to keep in touch with reliable bank-rating services to make sure your bank(s) continue to qualify for a high safety rating. Many U.S. banks, moreover, are at risk in ways that even the best ratings firms may be unable to recognize or track. To illustrate the problem, consider that Lehman Brothers Commercial Bank was rated B+ on a list dated 6/30/08 from one of our recommended rating services. Just a few months after that list was published, Lehman filed for bankruptcy.

Because of such uncertainty, banks in general are not the safest place to put the bulk of your money right now. Some smaller U.S. banks have been better at staying out of trouble, but size alone is not a guide to solvency. People of lesser means who must bank in risky systems in their home territory should keep, even in relatively strong local banks, only enough money on deposit to cover living expenses and whatever additional funds you trust the bank to hold.

If, despite all your precautions, you come to suspect that any of your chosen banks face the risk of closure, move your money to a safer bank immediately. If you cannot identify a safer bank, then do not hesitate to withdraw all of your money in cash. If you are not first in line, you may forfeit the opportunity.

Safe Banking Worldwide

A free market in banking would provide every imaginable service, from 100 percent safekeeping for a fee to 100 percent lending with a large potential return. To preserve their reputations, bankers would have an incentive to be extremely careful with your money. Monopoly money and regulated banking have produced quite a different result. Nevertheless, there still exist a few banks in the world that mainly provide a wealth preservation service as opposed to interest income and daily transactional conveniences. If you want the utmost safety for capital storage, if a bit less convenience, you must use such banks. The safest banking institutions in the world reside in countries that (1) do not have, and are unlikely to impose, exchange controls or wealth transfer restrictions and (2) have a low ratio of illiquid debts to deposits. Not surprisingly, the top candidates are the same as those with the safest debt: Switzerland and Singapore.

Nevertheless, do not fall into the trap of choosing a bank just because it's Swiss. Today's largest Swiss banks, with their fat portfolios of derivatives, are at immense risk of failure if a depression occurs. Furthermore, they have branches worldwide and are thus vulnerable to the whims of numerous governments. The best course of action is to locate smaller, safer local Swiss banks. Austria's low debt per capita makes it a good backup alternative. If you want to find a safe bank, these jurisdictions are the place to begin.

Using stringent rating requirements, SafeWealth Group has identified depository institutions that earn its highest rating for survivability in a global depression. The firm looks for banks with an unusually high net liquid equity ratio (i.e., the percentage of a bank's capital that is freely accessible), a low derivatives to capital ratio, a low level of derivatives held for the bank's account on a speculative basis and a low amount of deposits held at other banks.

If you are serious about safety and can meet a recommended bank's account minimum. SafeWealth Group can help you cut through red tape to establish relationships with such banks and other institutions. The reason you need to go through a representative is that these private Swiss banks do not readily accept accounts from any individual, corporation or trust representative that walks through the door, a policy that reflects their general conservatism. They will accept a new account only if its ownership and purpose are completely above board and will not endanger the bank's reputation. If you meet these standards, SafeWealth Group can secure the proper introductions for you and guide you through the process. If you seek a money manager as well, Hillier Capital can place your money in similar institutions through its already-established accounts. (See the Appendix for contact information and minimums.) If you are a Swiss or Singaporean resident and have ready access to such institutions, by all means stay put as long as local politics remain stable.

Act While You Can

When it comes to safety, it is always best to act early. Due largely to aggressive governmental policing of illegal activities such as the drug trade, money laundering, tax evasion and terrorist financing, average honest people do not enjoy the free, ready access to financial institutions that they did two decades ago. Some banks are now obliged to meet with prospective clients in person to satisfy suitability rules. There can be little doubt that if a crisis climate comes to pass, you could face many more obstacles if not outright denial of service. If you are truly intent on preserving your wealth, you should resist the temptation to procrastinate under the presumption that you can rely on the status quo. Opportunities close down all the time. For example, the two safest banks in London no longer accept non-British clients. In the U.S., the bank ranked the safest in the nation a few years ago no longer takes out-of-state accounts. A few of my prudent subscribers got in after I recommended it, but now the procrastinators have to look elsewhere. These are lessons. Don't delay, or the institutions now available to protect your savings may close their doors to you.

Once you move the bulk of your investment funds into the safest cash equivalents, and after you have chosen a safe bank or two for savings and transactions, then and only then should you consider speculating in the stock market with a small portion of your capital. That is the subject of the next chapter.

Chapter 17:

Should You Speculate in Stocks?

Uncomfortable woman in car: "I'm sitting on something!"
W.C. Fields: "I lost mine in the stock market."

—*International House* (1933)

Perhaps the number one precaution to take at the start of a deflationary crash is to make sure that your investment capital is *not* invested "long" in stocks, stock mutual funds, stock index futures, stock options, ETFs or any other equity-based investment or speculation. That advice alone should be worth the time you spent reading this book.

Don't presume that the Fed will rescue the stock market. The Japanese central bank has been aggressively buying shares of Japanese stocks for years to little result and will soon be stuck with wilting investments. In theory, the Fed could declare a support price for certain stocks, but which ones? And how much money would it commit to buying them? If the Fed were actually to buy equities or stock-index futures, the temporary result might be a brief rally, but the ultimate result would be a collapse in the value of the Fed's own assets when the market turned back down, making the Fed look foolish and compromising its primary goals, as cited in Chapter 10. It wouldn't want to keep repeating that experience. The bankers' pools of 1929 gave up on this strategy, and so will the Fed if it tries it.

Short Selling Stocks and Trading in Futures and Options

Short selling stocks or stock index futures contracts is a great strategy at the onset of a deflationary depression. The key to making a lot of money on the short side of a financial market while reducing risk as a bear market progresses is to be at maximum leverage near the top, thereafter increasing the size of the position while decreasing the ratio of leverage, which allows you to weather the inevitable big rallies. Nobody knows this.

The problem with applying this knowledge is that risk is huge if you are wrong. You also must avoid shorting special situations such as defense and natural resource stocks, which can move counter-trend, or at least fall less precipitously, when international tensions rise. Buying puts and "leaps," which are long-term puts, on stocks and stock indexes, will pay off in a bear market, but only if you time your purchase perfectly, as time is the enemy of a long-options position. You will not succeed on your first try, I guarantee. If you do not already know what the terms "puts" and "leaps" mean, I recommend that you avoid engaging in such activities.

If you are nevertheless determined to trade the markets, consider signing up for Todd Gordon's live-trading service at www.tradinganalysis.com. Todd is an experienced trader who uses the Wave Principle to identify what he deems to be high-probability setups in the markets and shows you how to manage risks using options strategies. He puts on his positions—while you watch—using his own money, in real time, and then manages the positions and explains why he is making each adjustment. You can watch Todd operate via high-definition video and, if you agree with him, you can take the same actions in your own portfolio. We liked Todd's service so much we recently partnered with him.

Finally, if you want to learn to do it yourself, there is no better series of instructional videos and trading courses than those by EWI's own Jeff Kennedy and Wayne Gorman. Jeff is our commodities analyst, and Wayne is a lifelong trader and former manager of trading desks at Citibank and Westpac. You can find these offerings at www.elliottwave.com/videos and www.elliottwave.com/on-demand-courses.

Unfortunately, there could well be *structural* risks in dealing with stocks and associated derivatives during a major retrenchment. Trading stocks, options and futures could be extremely problematic during a stock market panic. One reason is that trading platforms tend to break down when volume surges. When the exchange floor became a hurricane of paper on October 28 and 29, 1929, it took days to sort out who had bought and sold what and then determine whether investors and traders could afford to pay for their losses. You can experience the turmoil vicariously in any good history of the 1929 crash. To give you a flavor of what goes on, read this description, from one of my subscribers, of the tumult during a far milder panic:

> I worked for Merrill Lynch in New York in 1962 during the collapse. I well recall the failure of the teletype in our office and inexperienced clerks calling in the orders to the main office. I recall many of the screw-ups: buys called in as sells and vice versa. Some stocks had nicknames like Bessie (Bethlehem Steel), Peggy (Public Service Electric and Gas), and I recall the clerks calling in the orders by the stocks' nicknames and the person on the other end not knowing what the hell they were talking about. All the while, the market was collapsing.

Do you think investors and brokers will behave differently now that so much stock trading is done online? I don't. Do you think the experience will be smoother because modern computers are involved? I don't. In fact, today's system — much improved, to be sure — is nevertheless a recipe for an even bigger mess during a panic. Investors will be so nervous that they will screw up their orders. Huge volume will clog website servers, disrupting orders entered on-line. Orders may go in, but confirmations may not come out. A trader *might not know* if his sale or purchase went through. Is he in or out? Quote systems will falter at just the wrong time. Phone lines from you to the broker and from the broker to the floor will be jammed, and some will go down. Computer technicians will be working overtime while being distracted worrying about their own investments. Brokers and computer technicians will be operating on little sleep and at peak agitation. Customers will be entering orders wrong. Firms and regulators will begin to enact and enforce tighter restrictions on trading and margin. Price gaps will trigger stops at prices beyond the ability of some account holders to pay. You, the wise short seller, could survive all these problems only to discover that your broker has gone bankrupt or has been shut down or that its associated bank has had a computer breakdown or that its assets are depleted or frozen.

Unless you are prepared for such an environment, don't get suckered into this maelstrom thinking that the bear market will be business as usual, just in the other direction. If you want to try making a killing being short in the collapse, make sure that you are not overexposed. Make sure that if the system locks up for days or weeks, you will not be in a panic yourself. Make sure that in a worst-case scenario, the funds you place at risk are funds you could lose.

Inverse Index ("Short") Mutual Funds

Many people choose to invest in inverse index funds, also called short funds or bear funds, which are bets on falling stock prices. In this category, there are several standard index funds and over 100 exchange-traded funds (ETFs).

Sounds great, right? Well, things aren't that simple. You need to understand something important about how these short funds work. Holders of shares make money depending upon the short-term *percentage change* that the market undergoes *each day or half day*. This fact profoundly affects the outcome of your position.

In a persistently trending market, this situation is better than a short sale. Theoretically, the market can go down one percent per day indefinitely. If the market were to fall a long way in a straight line, these funds could compound your return beyond that of a normal short sale, which at most can gain 100%. Also, while the shares of these funds lose value in an up market, they do not quickly lose all of their value, as a short sale can when a stock doubles.

On the other hand, this attribute in some circumstances can present a big problem. To understand it, follow this example: You invest $100,000 in a doubly leveraged short S&P 500 fund with the index at 1000, which is a $200,000 short S&P 500 exposure. The next day, the index rises 10%, so you have lost $20,000. The short fund automatically resets your exposure to twice your equity at the end of the day, so your new exposure is short $160,000. The next day, the index returns to 1000, but your equity rises only to $94,545 because the percentage decline from the higher level is only 9.09 percent, and you didn't have enough exposure on the way back to make up your initial loss. The index is unchanged, but you lost money. The same negative result occurs when the index initially goes your way and then returns to its starting point. Critics call this attribute "beta slippage." This problem is compounded when markets are in a trading range, further when the inverse fund is leveraged, and even further for funds that reset twice a day. Since markets tend to fluctuate a lot, this is an especially negative attribute for long-term investors. The "beta slippage" described here for inverse index funds has proved to be a bigger issue than most people, including the fund managers themselves, expected. Inverse funds track the market exceptionally well day by day but not over the long term, especially in choppy and volatile markets. I found out the hard way. I held shares of a short fund in 2007-2009, and at the end of the biggest bear market since the Great Depression my gains were far less than implied by the change in stock prices. For a good explanation of the slippage problem, see www.altenergystocks.com/archives/2009/02/ultrapromises_fall_short.

To avoid the slippage problem and make these funds work in all environments, you have to be a short-term market timer. Being a successful one when you are restricted to trading in and out only once or twice a day *at a particular time* is nearly impossible.

There is a structural problem, too, in that inverse funds are derivatives dependent upon the ability of the managers to have their funds track the underlying indexes. In a chaotic environment, this task could prove impossible. In sum, I am not a fan of inverse index funds.

Managed Bear Funds

One option to consider is a portfolio of short or hedged stocks, managed by an expert. Actively managed bearish stock funds are designed to benefit from a declining stock market. There are very few around today because the stock mania has driven most of them out of business. A few courageous money managers have maintained this alternative. Two of the Gabelli funds fit this description.

The Comstock Capital Value Fund is positioned to profit from a declining market with a combination short-term debt securities, index puts and short sales. One of the funds' managers, Charles Minter, writes commentary, which you can read for free on their website.

Another bear fund is the GAMCO Mathers Fund. Manager Henry van der Eb takes a conservative approach, investing in Treasury debt, stocks hedged with options or futures, and short sales.

For information on these funds, contact the following:

Comstock Capital Value Fund
Managers: Charles Minter and Dennis DeCore
Website: www.comstockfunds.com
Email: info@comstockfunds.com
Address: 24 S. Main St, Yardley PA 19067
Phone: 215-493-7076
Fax: 215-493-8083
Minimum $1000

GAMCO Mathers Fund
Manager: Henry van der Eb, CFA
Website: www.gabelli.com

Email: info@gabelli.com
Address: One Corporate Center, Rye NY 10580
Phone: 800-422-3554
Minimum: $1000

Managers Who Are Not Afraid To Be Bearish

John Hussman of the Hussman Funds offers three stock funds and a bond fund. They can be bullishly or bearishly oriented, but when markets appear overpriced, Hussman says so in no uncertain terms and positions accordingly. He offers analytical commentary free on his website:

Hussman Funds
Manager: John Hussman, PhD
Website: www.hussmanfunds.com
Phone: 800-487-7626; 513-326-3551
Minimum $1000/$500 for IRAs

You can also find portfolio managers who are not afraid to be bearish. I personally know of only a few, and they may or may not be the best. In the U.S., examples are Lang Asset Management (www.langasset.com), a small firm that selects medium-to-large-cap stocks that look overpriced and shorts them, sometimes hedging with options or by other means. In Asia, Marc Faber Ltd. (www.gloomboomdoom.com), and in Europe, Zulauf Asset Management AG (Grafenauweg 4, CH-6300 Zug, Switzerland; www.felixzulauf.com, phone: (US: 011) 41-41-724-5701), provide bearishly oriented management. Minimum funding requirements range between $100,000 and $3 million.

To find more leads, check out the Hedge Fund Association at http://www.hedgefundassoc.org. Hedge funds are only as good as their managers. Some fund managers use huge leverage and can "blow up," losing everything on bad bets. The more spectacular of those make the newspapers; there are others that just go quietly. If you want to go this route, choose wisely and make sure that you satisfy yourself that the money manager you choose deals with safe banks. I have not investigated that aspect of any of these funds.

Temporary Opportunity?

The opportunity to make money on the downside in a deflationary crash can hardly be overstated, because *you will be making more dollars as the value of dollars* is soaring. It's a double benefit. Will it always be there?

I recall only one time when authorities banned buying in a bull market. The Comex futures exchange banned orders "to open" in silver futures in January 1980 to save their own skins, since many exchange members were short. Most investors were long, so their only allowed course was to sell. By changing the rules, the exchange profited and investors got killed. (For more on that story, read *Silver Bonanza*, by James Blanchard and Franklin Sanders, published by Jefferson Financial, 2400 Jefferson Highway, Suite 600, Jefferson, LA 70121, phone 504-837-3033.)

In a bear market, bullish investors always come to believe that short sellers are "driving the market down," when in fact the decline is almost entirely due to selling from within their own over-invested ranks. Sometimes authorities outlaw selling stocks short. In doing so, they remove the one class of investors that *must* buy. Every short sale (except when stocks go to zero) must be *covered*, i.e., the stock must be purchased to close the trade. A ban on short selling creates a market with no latent buying power at all, making it even less liquid than it was. Then it can slip lower day after day, unhindered by the buying of nervous shorts. Like all other bans on free exchange, a ban on short selling hurts those whom it is designed to help.

If authorities in your country decide to disallow short selling, the bad news is that this option will be closed to you. The good news is that they usually take such actions near major bottoms, so it will probably be about time to cover shorts and start composing your "buy" list anyway.

Chapter 18:

Should You Invest in Commodities?

Figures 18-1 through 18-9 show what happened to commodity prices from 1929 through 1938. Pay particular attention to what happened in 1929-1932, the three years of intense deflation in which the stock market crashed. As you can see, commodities crashed, too.

You can pofit by being short commodity futures in a deflationary crash. This is a player's game, though, and I am not about to urge a typical investor to follow that course. If you are a seasoned commodity trader, avoid the long side and use rallies to sell short. Make sure your broker keeps your liquid funds in T-bills or an equally safe medium.

There can be exceptions to the broad trend. A commodity can rise against the trend on a war, a war scare, a shortage or a disruption of transport.

Some people today who are concerned about economic upset are looking for a replay of the inflationary 1970s, in which commodities rose. But most assets will be moving down more or less together as liquidity contracts. Any deflation will crush hard-asset prices right along with share prices, just as it always has.

Prices of Commodities, 1929 — 1938

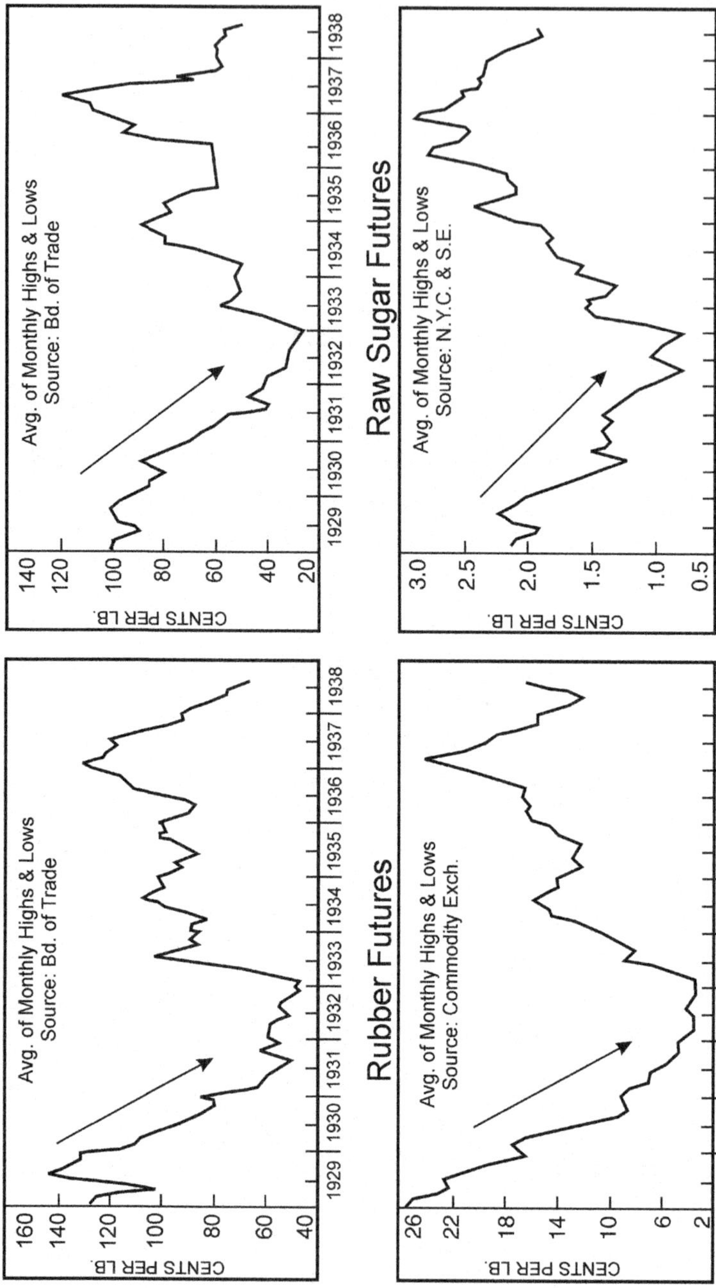

Figure 18-1 through 18-4

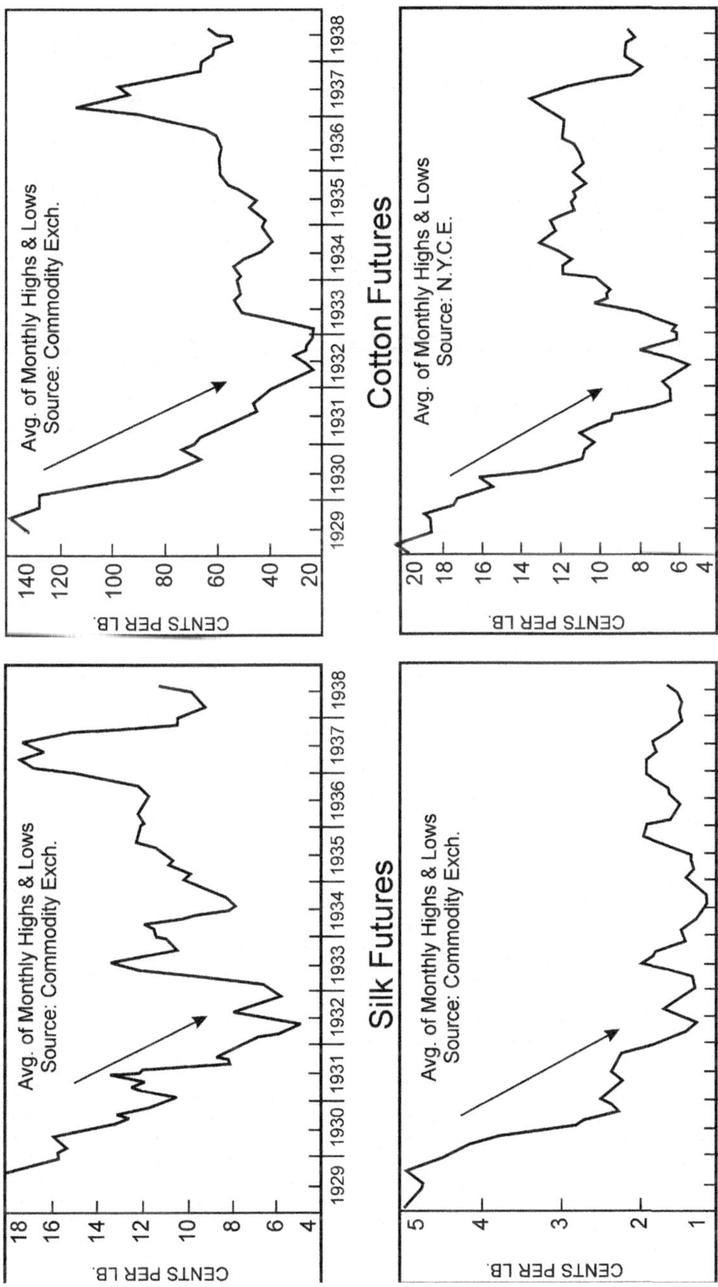

Figure 18-5 through 18-8

Scrap Steel
Mid-Month Quote
Source: Iron Age
CENTS PER LB.
22
20
18
16
14
12
10
8
6
1929
1930
1931
1932
1933
1934
1935
1936
1937
1938

Figure 18-9

Chapter 19:

Should You Invest in Precious Metals or Cryptocurrencies?

Precious metals may one day to become the most important asset class to own. Since currencies today are etherial, it is likely that sometime during this century people will question the validity of the fiat money system. The hard-money movement of the 1970s may prove to have been just a warm-up for fututre events. Governments may exercise powers to keep the fiat paper money system afloat, defending their currencies with various schemes and legal restrictions, but in the end, gold will win.

Why is gold such a desirable commodity? At the top of the list is its impeccable utility as a store of value. Relentless inflating has caused chronic value losses in currencies. The U.S. dollar has dropped in value by 98.5% since the Fed came into being. Its collapse in value has compromised the financial security of the working class, the middle class and retirees. Had modern money a tangible basis, then workers could have saved for their retirement in a true store of value, and retirees would have far more buying power in their golden years. It is already a pity to observe hard-working people unable to save a penny. It will be heart wrenching to see innocent people suffer during the ultimate resolution of governments' and central banks' credit-expansion policies. Using gold as money contributes to long-run productive stability. By setting up governments' and central banks with monopoly powers dedicated to paper money, governments traded that stability for an international casino in which money manipulators thrive at the expense of producers and savers.

It is dangerous to entrust any service crucial to survival to a statutory monopoly or government regulation. When the Russian government handled food production and distribution, central planners reported over seven straight decades of "bad weather" and food shortages. Similarly, central bankers have presided over decades of rising prices, monetary debasement and the impoverishment of savers. Periodic credit inflation would occur in a free market as well, but its effects would be limited because real money cannot be inflated, and prudent people and institutions could choose to opt out of a credit binge in favor of holding real money. A free people would choose the best money, and I have no doubt that it would be gold.

Is the Precious Metals' Bear Market Over?

Despite the verity of gold as the best form of money, there is a right time for everything. Advisors who have declared inflation's inevitability kept their followers in gold and silver for 21 years, from 1980 to 2001, as they plummeted 70% and 93% respectively in dollar terms, even while the dollar was losing purchasing power at the local store. They have done it again in the bear market since 2011, during which gold and silver have fallen as much as 45% and 73%, respectively, and they are still down 33% and 66%. Those losses, even forgetting the massive opportunity costs, have been staggering.

Right now, I think it likely that gold and silver will fall into their final dollar price lows at the bottom of the deflation because that is what happened to silver in the last great deflation. Figure 19-1 shows that although silver had undergone most of its bear market by the time of the 1929 high in the stock market, it still followed commodities and paper assets down during the deflation to a final low in December 1932. There is rarely sufficient

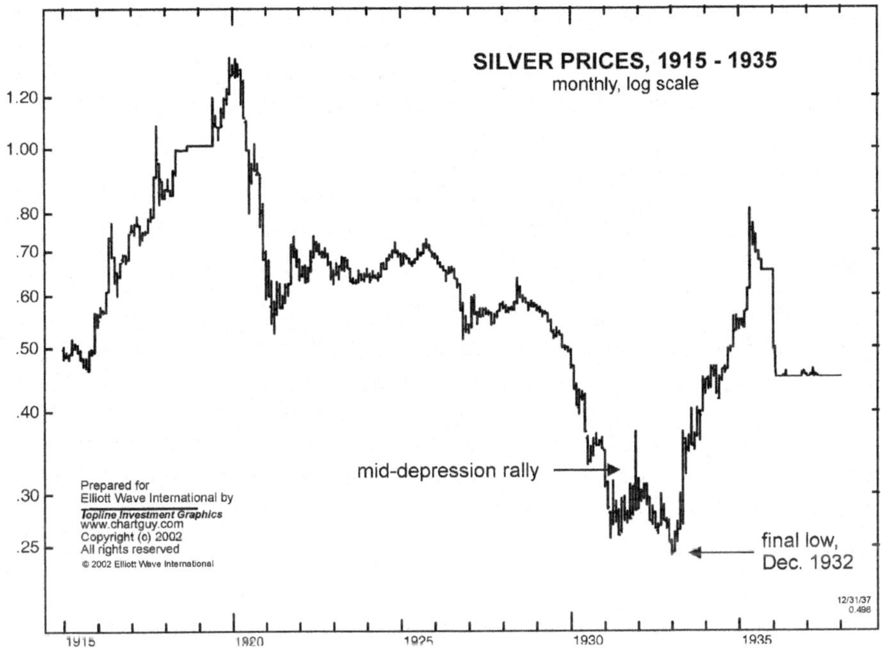

Figure 19-1

reason to bet heavily on cycles doing something different from what they have done in the past, and this cycle's history implies that the precious metals' bear market is not over yet. If the coming deflation acts like the last one, then at its end we will have a great buying opportunity for gold and silver — maybe the greatest ever.

Most gold bugs today assert that gold and silver are a "deflation hedge," a "war hedge," and a "depression hedge," claims that the record does not convincingly support. The price history of 1931 is instructive in showing that there was a year-long mid-depression rally in the price of silver, which ended on a spike, indicating brief panic buying. Investors of that time were undoubtedly convinced that silver would provide counter-trend solace during monetary difficulty. They were remembering silver's positive performance during the preceding difficult times of 1914-1919, which were inflationary. Similarly, today's precious metals enthusiasts expect a replay of the inflationary 1970s, but once again deflation will be the problem.

The claim that people "rushed into gold" in the early 1930s has been a mainstay of the gold advocates' argument. They rarely tell the whole story. Some people may have bought gold then because the U.S. government had fixed the price, at $20.67 per ounce. As prices for everything else plunged, gold was soaring in relative value. Who wouldn't want to own it? If the government had fixed the price of any other substance, people would have invested in that instead. But gold did not go *up* during that time, and, as noted above, silver went down. As with the price of silver in the 1930s, the price of gold today is unfixed. It is free to trade at market price, which means that it can go down during a dollar deflation. I cannot guarantee that it will; I can only state that there is no good case to be made that history indicates otherwise.

Buy Gold and Silver Anyway

You might be surprised to find that I advocate holding a healthy amount of gold and silver anyway. There are several reasons for this stance:

First, it could be different this time, for some reason I cannot foresee. In a world of fiat currencies, prudence demands hedging one's position and beating any future rush to tangible money.

Second, these metals should perform well on a relative basis compared to most other investments. Many stocks and bonds will go to zero, but precious metals won't.

Third, the metals should soar once the period of deflation is over. Notice in Figure 19-1 that silver rebounded ferociously after it bottomed in 1932, tripling in just two years, eventually rewarding those who continued to hold it. In 1934, the government began a long campaign of fixing the price of newly mined silver, though each level was temporary and closely reflected market forces. If deflation again brings precious metals prices down, the rebound after the bottom should be no less robust. Given the potential for politically motivated inflation, it could well be much stronger. So, by all means, you want to own precious metals prior to the onset of the post-depression recovery.

Finally, if you buy gold and silver now, *you'll have it*. If investors worldwide panic into hard assets, locking up supplies, if governments ban gold sales, you won't be stuck entirely in paper currency. You will already own something that everyone else wants.

Be aware that the present legalities of gold and silver ownership could change. This political risk isn't fantasy, even in the Land of the Free. In 1933, President Roosevelt outlawed gold ownership for U.S. citizens and imposed a ten-year prison sentence on people who refused to surrender their gold to a Federal Reserve Bank within 25 days. The ban on gold stayed in place for over four decades, until President Ford lifted it on the first day of 1975.

Should you buy gold and silver now? If you are willing to see the dollar value of the precious metals drop substantially before they rise, then I would say, that's the price you're willing to pay for its current availability, the added breadth in your portfolio and for the "insurance" against an unexpected inflation scenario. If you want to arrange for capital safety in every way that you can manage, then diversification into real money is a necessary part of that effort.

How To Buy Gold and Silver

I do not advocate buying gold and silver in paper form by way of futures contracts, ETFs, gold-backed bonds from a government or ownership certificates connected to commingled accounts at storage facilities. After all, which is better — owning actual gold or some entity's promise to pay it? For maximum safety, you should own gold and silver in physical form, outright.

One-kilo bars are widely traded globally, but "standard bars" of 400 fine ounces are the primary form of gold and silver used by central banks and recognized by the U.S. Comex, the London Bullion Market Association and the Tokyo Commodity Exchange (TOCOM). So, that is the most liquid medium for storing substantial wealth in gold.

Coins are a good medium for smaller portfolios. Everyone should own a share of coins, because some day tangible money could once again become a medium of exchange, at least temporarily. The best-known and most liquid "bullion" style gold coins are American Eagles, South African Krugerrands, Canadian Maple Leafs, Australian Nuggets and Austrian Coronas. As for silver, Americans should own a bag or two of circulated U.S. silver coins. Most coin dealers can get you these items. After you have a core position, accumulate more metals at a pace with which you are comfortable, preferably on price declines.

Although collectibility premiums have shrunk a lot since 1989, you should still avoid coins that cost more due to rarity. Many dealers recommend paying up for rare coins because in 1933 collectible gold coins were exempt from U.S. government confiscation. The cutoff point for rarity was never codified, though, and there is little reason to expect that exactly the same law will go into effect in the future. If a government outlaws gold again, the jig will be up on buying goods with your collectible gold coins anyway, so what's the point of having them? At that point, I would rather have a cache of pre-1965 U.S. silver coins for everyday trade.

It is not a good idea to invest in gold stocks. In common-stock bear markets, stocks of gold mining companies have more often gone down than up except during relatively rare five to ten-year bull markets in commodities. Few people know that from the top day in the Dow in 1929 to the bottom day in 1932, gold mining shares rose only slightly *even though the U.S. government propped up the companies' product by fixing its price.* Mining shares did not soar in value until the stock market as a whole turned up in July 1932. Today the government does not fix the price of gold, so in the deflation we currently face, gold mines will enjoy no false advantage over any other companies. Their stocks will probably rally when the overall stock market rallies, but they have no built-in support as they did in the 1930s, so they are likely to disappoint those who invest in them. (Of course, if the government's policy on gold changes, then so might the outlook for mining share prices.) Also be aware that there are risks to the independence of mining companies. Owning gold shares means betting that no government will nationalize the mines whose shares you own. When deflation is raging, political tensions are at their most severe.

In 1933, Roosevelt's Executive Order stated, "Your possession of these proscribed metals and/or your maintenance of a safe-deposit box to store them is known to the Government from bank and insurance records. Therefore, be advised that your vault box must remain sealed, and may only be opened in the presence of an agent of The Internal Revenue Service." Most banks were only too happy to comply with this order because gold prohibition promised their salvation, or so they believed. If your government decides to confiscate gold — say, to fight the drug trade or terrorism — your country's banks will probably be recruited in the operation. By the way, this potential is a good reason to refrain from keeping any important personal papers in bank safe deposit boxes in any jurisdiction where such an action is possible. Otherwise, you may have to wait a while for permission to access the contents.

If you want to buy at least $100,000 worth of gold and/or silver bars and store them in one or more of the safest depositories in the world, contact SafeWealth Group. If you want to buy bullion-style gold coins or circulated silver coins inside the U.S. and store them domestically, check out the dealers listed below. (Fidelitrade also offers an exchange-approved depository.) Be sure to cross-check prices before buying.

Fidelitrade
President: Jonathon Potts
Website: www.fidelitrade.com
Email: info@fidelitrade.com
Address: 3601 North Market Street,
Wilmington, DE 19802
Phone: 800-223-1080 and 302-762-6200
Fax: 302-762-2902

Hancock & Harwell
President: Robert L. Harwell
Website: www.raregold.com
Email: info@raregold.com
Address: Suite 310, 3155 Roswell Rd.,
Atlanta, GA 30305
Phone: 404-261-6565

Investment Rarities, Inc.
President: James R. Cook
Website: www.investmentrarities.com
Email: contact@investmentrarities.com
Address: 7850 Metro Parkway
Bloomington, MN 55425-1521
Phone: 800-328-1860 and 952-853-0700

Miles Franklin Ltd.
President: Andrew Schectman
Website: www.milesfranklin.com
Email: andy@milesfranklin.com
Address: 801 Twelve Oaks Center Drive, Suite 834,
Wayzata, MN 55391
Phone: 800-822-8080 and 952-929-7006
Fax: 952-476-7971

Straight Talk Assets, Inc.
President: Glenn R. Fried
Website: www.coinmoney.com
Email: straighttalk@mindspring.com
Address: P.O. Box 1301, Gainesville, GA 30503
Phone: 800-944-9249 and 770-536-8045

Well-heeled investors should round out their holdings with platinum. Platinum is a precious metal, and in recent decades, its coinage has established it as an emerging monetary metal as well.

Platinum has several advantages over gold and silver, not the least of which is that it packs more value per ounce. If you can afford to diversify to this extent, ask your metals dealer about platinum bars and coins.

GoldMoney is another option. GoldMoney stores customers' gold, silver, platinum and palladium in fully insured vaults in London, Zurich, Hong Kong, Singapore and Toronto. External auditors ensure that the company has the metal that it credits to you. GoldMoney never lends its deposits, which means that, unlike a bank, it can never become a participant in a credit bubble and thereby subject to a bust. An account with GoldMoney is not the same as having physical metal in your hands, but that is both a drawback and an advantage. If you have to leave your jurisdiction someday due to political unrest, you won't have to figure out how to get your gold out, too. All you have to do is remember your account number. And if you do wish to hold physical gold, GoldMoney will ship your gold in bar form to virtually any requested location.

Be aware that, as for all institutions, adverse events such as political aggression could endanger any storage company's holdings. Make sure you satisfy yourself that opening this type of account is the right thing to do. Here is GoldMoney's contact information:

GoldMoney
Director: Geoff Turk
Website: www.goldmoney.com
Address: Net Transactions Limited, 1st Floor,
32 Commercial Street, St. Helier
Jersey, JE2 3RU, British Channel Islands
Phone: (U.S. & Canada) 855-583-4653
(UK & International) 44-1543-633-900
Fax: (U.S. dial 011) 44-1534-633-901

Crytocurrencies

What about cryptocurrencies? Should you store money in them? Elliott Wave International was the first financial publishing firm, by years, to feature an enthusiastic write-up on the idea of cryptocurrency. Back in September 2010, *The Elliott Wave Theorist* published three pages by Elliott Prechter on bitcoin, which was selling then for only six cents. When it passed $3000, he began warning that bitcoin was late in an investment mania. When it passed $20,000, he publicly warned of a "risk of collapse," immediately after which the prices for bitcoin and its clones began falling. Sadly, cryptocurrencies had become the focus of yet another financial mania, thereby eliminating them, for the time being, from consideration as a good store of value.

Practically speaking, bitcoin has a big advantage over gold. Gold is too heavy to carry around, but you can go anywhere and retain quick access to a store of bitcoins. Bitcoin also has a big advantage over state-run currencies, which is that is cannot be inflated. So, why is this not a top choice for holding wealth? The answer is that if someone, someday, were to come out with a superior technology—which in fact seems likely—bitcoins could end up at zero value. The current blockchain on which bitcoin is dependent has become slow and cumbersome while simultaneously requiring huge amounts of energy to maintain, making it unsuitable for everyday transactions and ripe for either improvement or replacement.

The Newest Idea: Gold-Backed Digital Cash

A brand-new idea combines the time-honored monetary value of gold with the modern idea of cryptocurrency. Half a dozen firms have recently cooperated to create a blockchain-based platform called VaultChain, developed by TradeWind Markets, for trading bits of ownership in physical gold, which will be stored in vaults at the Royal Canadian Mint. A similar arrangement is in place between CME Group and the U.K.'s Royal Mint.

Essentially, this is a new form of old money: *gold-backed, digital cash*, which users will hold in cyberwallets similar to those used for holding bitcoins. Dealers will be charged fees, but in contrast to the high cost of trading physical gold today, everyday users will be charged no transaction fees. This is an attractive, real-money alternative to unbacked cybercurrencies. If it becomes popular, long-time gold hoarders will finally own widely recognized real money. Rather than perform new work to obtain the digital form, they might opt to trade their physical gold for it.

No form of money, however, is drawback-free, and neither is this one. Its weakness is that, while bitcoins are decentralized and mostly immune to bulk seizure, any sufficiently powerful entity could seize the entire stock of gold that backs this new digital currency. To reduce this risk, its proponents will have to find a way to distribute the physical backing in locations around the world or employ some other means of protecting the gold that backs the currency.

Chapter 20:

Pensions, Insurance and Annuities

What To Do With Your Pension Plan

The bull market in stocks has gone on so long that pension funds, formerly boasting conservative portfolios, have embraced stocks as a safe investment. Over half of the value of public pension funds is committed to stock shares. This is a setup for disaster.

Equally dangerous, banks and mortgage companies lend money to consumers via credit cards, auto loans and mortgages and then package and re-sell those loans as investments to pension funds as well as portfolio managers, insurance companies and even trust departments at other banks. The issuing banks keep most of the interest paid by the consumers in exchange for guaranteeing an interest payment (today about 3¼%) on the package. These investments are called "securitized loans," and banks and mortgage companies have issued $10 trillion worth of them. This high sum implies that if you have a managed trust, invest in a debt fund or have insurance or a pension, you are almost surely dependent upon some of these deals.

When banks sell the packages, they get back as much money as they lent out in the first place, so guess what. They can go right out and roll the same percentage of their deposits out again and again as new consumer loans. Investors in the packages are the ultimate creditors.

If the issuing banks get in trouble some day and can't pay, the owners of the debt packages will then have dibs on the interest payments from the consumers. If those payments dry up, they have that great collateral to fall back on: vacant homes, used cars and household junk. If a depression is on, what will that collateral be worth?

If such deals don't sound that solid to you, then why are so many institutions making these investments? Because they're buying them with OPM: Other People's Money...your money. And besides, it's "guaranteed" and backed by "collateral"!

This scheme, like so many others in existence today, works only as long as the debtors and the economy can keep up the pace of interest payments. For credit cards, interest rates commonly run about 20%. The median penalty rate, which is not limited by law, is a crippling 30%. In a major economic downturn, such debts will be unsustainable.

Make sure you fully understand all aspects of your government's *individual* retirement plans as well. In the U.S., this includes such structures as IRAs, 401Ks and Keoghs. If you anticipate severe system-wide financial and political stresses, you may decide to liquidate any such plans and pay whatever penalty is required. Why? Because there are strings attached to the perk of having your money sheltered from taxes. You may do only what the government allows you to do with the money. It restricts certain investments and can change the list at any time. It charges a penalty for early withdrawal and can change the amount of the penalty at any time, too.

What is the worst that could happen? In Argentina, the government continued to spend more than it took in until it went broke trying to pay the interest on its debt. In December 2001, it seized $2.3 billion dollars worth of deposits in *private pension funds* to pay its bills.

In the 1930s, the world heard a lot of populist rhetoric about why "rich" people should be plundered for the public good. It is easy to imagine such talk in the next crisis, directed at requiring wealthy people to forfeit their retirement savings for the good of the nation.

With the retirement setup in the U.S., the government need not be as direct as Argentina's. It need merely assert, after a stock market fall decimates many people's savings, that stocks are too risky to hold for retirement purposes. Under the guise of protecting you, it could ban stocks and perhaps other investments in tax-exempt pension plans and restrict assets to one category: "safe" long-term U.S. Treasury bonds. Then it could raise the penalty of early withdrawal to 100%. Bingo. The government will have seized the entire $2 trillion — or what's left of it given a crash — that today is held in government-sponsored, tax-deferred private pension plans. I'm not saying it will happen, but it could, and wouldn't you rather have your money safely under your own discretion?

By the way, if you are normally in a high tax bracket and find yourself in a year with zero income or significant business losses, you can cash out part or all of your plan with either less federal tax (since you will be in a lower tax bracket) or no federal tax, if your earned-income losses cancel out the income from the plan. If you are under the age of 59½, you will normally have to pay a penalty, which is currently 10% of the value of the distribution. If you use the funds to pay for college tuition, though, you can even avoid the penalty. Individual state tax laws differ on this issue. Be sure to consult a tax advisor before proceeding.

Perhaps you have no such opportunity for tax saving and do not want to pay the penalty attached to premature withdrawal. If your balance is high enough, you may wish to consider converting your retirement plan investments into an annuity at a safe insurance company, if you can find one (see upcoming discussion). It is highly likely — though not assured — that such investments would be left alone even in a national financial emergency.

If you have money in a personally directed corporate or government employee retirement plan with limited options and want to avoid risk in a deflationary depression, move it out of stock and bond funds. Park it in the safest money market fund available within the plan. Investigate the rules that pertain to cashing out and decide your next course of action.

If you or your family owns a small company and is the sole beneficiary of its pension or profit sharing plan, you should lodge its assets in a safe bank or money market fund. As an alternative, depending upon your age and requirements, you may consider converting it into an annuity, issued by a safe insurance company.

What To Do With Your Insurance and Annuities

If you believe that your fortunes are not dependent upon junk bonds, you might be in for a surprise. If you have life insurance, especially if you have a "guaranteed rate of return" insurance policy, your policy may be dependent upon the performance of junk bonds. Your insurance nest egg, to put it bluntly, may be at risk.

Some insurance companies guarantee a minimum return on "equity-indexed annuities" while letting you participate in the market's gains but not its losses. An article in a major financial magazine called these plans "a bear-proof way to ride the market" that "removes downside risk." But the way it's done does create risk, because the structure involves zero-coupon bonds, index options and other exotic vehicles. This scheme will surely blow up, and if it does, the guarantee will stress the insurance companies that sell these policies.

Even most conservatively run insurance companies are massively exposed to losses during a major deflation, because they invest in standard vehicles such as stocks, bonds and real estate.

A deflationary vise will put double pressure on the solvency of insurance companies. As the values of most investments fall, the value of insurance companies' portfolios will fall. Conversely, as the economy weakens, more and more people will decide to cash out their policies. Insurance companies become hard-pressed to honor the value of whole-life policies when there is a net outflow of cash at the same time that property and stock investments are declining in value.

When insurance companies implode, they file for bankruptcy, and you can be left out in the cold. I know, because my insurance broker placed our insurance with, of all the companies in the world, Confederation Life. In 1994, it collapsed, along with Baldwin United and First Executive Corporation, which were huge institutions. See what happened when I didn't do the necessary research? If you think you can rely on your broker to recommend a safe insurance company, think again. Brokers shop mainly for price, and when they do look into safety, they rely on rating services that don't do a good job (see Chapter 21). As it turned out, I was lucky. Government and industry leaders in both the U.S. and Canada worked for three years to distribute the policies to other companies. When my policy moved, it carried another full year's cash-out restriction, and troughout this lengthy process I was still required to pay the premiums. The only reason the deal finally made it through was that the North American financial boom resumed in the second half of the 1990s, and other insurance companies felt safe taking on the additional obligations. I cashed out the day I was able.

When a bust is in force, few insurance companies are willing or able to take over a stressed company's policy obligations, which may have little collateral behind them. If your insurance company fails, your investment of a lifetime will be gone. It's happened to many people and will happen to many more.

Whole-life policies are, while often necessary for family protection, are almost always a bad investment. During inflationary times, their real value grows far more slowly than it appears, if at all, because the purchasing power of the monetary unit declines. During deflationary times, the policy your family is counting on to protect against death or old age can disappear if the company fails.

One option is to cash out such policies and buy term insurance instead. With term insurance, you can keep an eye on the fortunes of various companies and switch from one to another. On the other hand, if you miss a renewal due to accident or illness, you're out of luck. Talk to your insurance broker about the courses of action open to you.

On the other hand, an interesting "deflation bonus" can also come available if you're careful. If you have whole-life insurance or an annuity with a *sound company*, you can actually come out way ahead because *the values and payouts are denominated in currency.* During deflation, the value of cash rises, so in terms of purchasing power, each dollar of value in your policy will be able to purchase more goods and services than it previously did. All you need to do is find a sound company.

Where To Buy Your Insurance Policies

At minimum, you should move your whole-life insurance policy or annuity to a sound insurer as soon as possible. If you delay too long in moving your policy and the company's assets are frozen, you will have no recourse.

As far as I can tell, Weiss Ratings, Inc. produces the most reliable ratings of U.S. insurance companies. Their system is also simple and straightforward. Unlike the maze of gradations such as "Bbb+" and so on that other services use, the Weiss system simply reads like a report card, from A+ down to F, adding only a set of "E" grades prior to F. Weiss considers any company rated B- or above to have "good" financial safety but recommends that you do business with companies rated B+ or better. In normal times, that assessment is probably all you need. However, if you believe that there is a reasonable risk of that rare and devastating event, a deflationary crash and depression, why not demand the absolute best?

Of course, as prudent as the judgments of a rating service may be, any such ratings do not fully take into account other considerations that will be crucial in a depression. For example, what bank(s) does your insurer use to hold its assets and make transactions? If an insurer's main bank implodes, its situation could become chaotic. This one factor could override even an insurer's A+ credit rating. Ratings can change for all sorts of reasons. For maximum confidence, keep abreast of Weiss' ratings as they pertain to the companies you choose but do you own research as well.

As if there were not already enough to worry about, the currency denomination of your policy may also prove crucial. If the currency in which you expect to be paid becomes hyperinflated and collapses in value, so will your plans for retirement. I do not consider this possibility an immediate risk, but it could come into play later, as suggested in Chapter 10.

The main point is to make sure that you assess the vulnerability of your insurance policies and annuities now. If you are satisfied, fine. If not, then you can take appropriate action before your insurance company, its bank, or you, become too stressed to adapt.

Chapter 21:

Reliable Sources for Financial Warnings

Safety Ratings for Financial Institutions

The most widely utilized rating services are almost always woefully late in warning you of problems within financial institutions. They often seem to get information about a company around the time that everyone else does, which means that the price of the associated stock or bond has already changed to reflect that information. In severe cases, a company can collapse before the standard rating services know what hit it. When all you can see is dust, they just skip the downgrading process and shift the company's rating from "investment grade" to "default" status.

Examples abound. The debt of the largest real estate developer in the world, Olympia & York of Canada, had an AA rating in 1991. A year later, it was bankrupt. Rating services missed the historic debacles at Barings Bank, Sumitomo Bank and Enron. Enron's bonds enjoyed an "investment grade" rating four days before the company went bankrupt. In my view, Enron's bonds were transparently junk well before their collapse. Why? Because the firm employed an army of traders in derivatives, which is an absolute guarantee of ultimate failure even when it's *not* a company's main business.

Sometimes there are structural reasons for the overvaluation of debt issues. For example, many investors bought the stock and debt offerings of Fannie Mae, Freddie Mac and the FHLBs because they thought the U.S. government guaranteed them. By law, it doesn't. Back in the early 2000s, these companies simply had the right to borrow money from the U.S. Treasury, $2.5 billion in the case of Fannie and Freddie and $4 billion in the case of the FHLBs. Because of this access to public funding, the bonds of these companies were exempt from SEC registration and disclosure requirements; they were simply *presumed* to be safe. But these credit lines ultimately represented less than ¼ of 1% of each company's outstanding mortgage loans, a drop in the bucket. Naturally, those rights proved to be grossly inadequate in the face of the housing crisis of 2006-2012. Before it was over, an embarrassed federal government had allowed Fannie Mae and Freddie Mac to borrow a combined total of 34 times the pledged amount: $103.8 billion and $65.2 billion, respectively. But even that largesse could not save the stock. Managers of these companies were shocked when the initial wave of the housing crises devastated their corporate earnings. Investors in these companies' stocks and bonds were caught off guard when their stock prices and bond ratings collapsed. Stockholders lost over 99% of their investment, as Fannie Mae and Freddie Mac shares fell from 2007 highs of $70.5 and $68.12 a share, respectively, to 18.5 and 12.8 cents per share (see Figure 13-2 in Chapter 13). Most rating services never saw the problem coming, either. Today, thanks to their special relationship with the U.S. Treasury, shares in both companies still trade for about $1.60 a share. These institutions will not likely survive the next wave of housing devaluation.

A few companies take a stringent approach to rating institutional safety. I listed three good U.S. bank and insurance-company rating firms in Chapters 16 and 20. Weiss Ratings, Inc. has quite reliable, detailed ratings on a broader range of U.S. institutions. For example, while most analysts never saw the Enron disaster coming, Weiss placed Enron on its "Corporate Earnings Blacklist" in April 2001 and cited the company as being "highly suspect of manipulating its earnings reports." Two quarters later, the scandal broke, and countless employees and investors — people who hadn't the foggiest notion about taking the precautions I'm suggesting to you in this book — lost everything.

Investment Advice from Brokers

Throughout my career, I have advised people not to trust a brokerage firm's "fundamental" (as opposed to technical) analysts to warn you about anything. Brokerage-firm analysts are notoriously poor at market timing. Besides being beholden to their corporate clients, which gives them an extreme bullish bias, most of these analysts use the wrong tools. Even when they are independent thinkers, they are rarely students of market psychology and thus have no idea how to figure out when a stock is probably topping. In fact, brokerage firm analysts are typically cheerleaders for a stock while it is topping out and during most of its fall. Over 20 years ago, when I worked as a Technical Market Specialist at Merrill Lynch, I watched as a fundamental analyst kept a "buy" rating on a maker of CB radios while its stock dropped from 19 to 1. Nothing has changed. According to reports, 11 out of 16 analysts covering Enron had a "buy" (some even emphasized "strong buy") on the stock four weeks before the company declared bankruptcy and well after the decline in the stock price had wiped out its investors. As most people have subsequently learned, brokerage firm analysts rarely use the word "sell." If they really think a company's stock is dangerous, they label it a "hold." The problem with trying to follow this guideline, though, is that they usually label a stock that way after its bear market has run most or all of its course. To avoid being hurt by these strategists, you need independent market analysis.

Technical Analysis Newsletters

Technicians are few and far between these days. In addition to my own company's publications (see Appendix), here are ten newsletters and services whose writers know market history, use supporting analysis, apply their disciplines with passion and care, and are variously bold or cautious depending upon what their work implies:

cycle analysis

Peter Eliades
Stockmarket Cycles
P.O. Box 606
Dunlap CA 93621 US
Phone: 707-769-4800
Website: www.stockmarketcycles.com
Email: peter@stockmarketcycles.com

Dow Theory and cycles

Tim Wood, CPA
Cycles News & Views
1545 Gulf Shores Parkway, PMB # 251
Gulf Shores, Alabama 36542
Phone: 504-208-9781
Website: www.cyclesman.com
Email: timwood1@cyclesman.com

seasonal, planetary and lunar influences

Christopher Carolan
The Spiral Calendar
Website: www.spiralcalendar.com
Email: chris@carolan.org

Arch Crawford
Crawford Perspectives
6890 East Sunrise Drive, Suite 70
Tucson, AZ 85750-0840
Phone: 520-577-1158
Website: www.crawfordperspectives.com
Email: crawfordperspectives@earthlink.net

Stephen Puetz
Universal Cycle Theory Financial Newsletter
Universal Cycle Theory
2233 Ala Wai Blvd 3-C
Honolulu, Hawaii 96815
Website: www.uct-news.com
Email: contact@uct-news.com

sentiment indicators

Jake Bernstein
Daily Sentiment Index
Phone: 800-678-5253, 831-430-0600
Website: www.trade-futures.com
Email: jake@trade-futures.com

Stephen Briese
Bullish Review
Insider Capital Group
Website: www.insidercapital.com

Jason Geopfert
Daily Sentiment Report
Sundial Capital Research
12527 Central Avenue NE, Suite 165
Blaine, MN 55434
Phone: 888-795-9893
Website: www.sentimentrader.com
Email: admin@sentimentrader.com

Jim Grey
Investors Intelligence
Chartcraft, Inc.
68 Walnut Rd.
Louisa, VA 23093
Phone: 877 322 4676
Website: www.investorsintelligence.com
Email: support@investorsintelligence.com

technical and credit-market analysis

Bert Dohmen
The Wellington Letter
Address: P.O. Box 492433
Los Angeles, CA 90049
Phone: 310-444-9090
Website: www.dohmencapital.com
Email: office@dohmencapital.com

If I were restricted to subscribing to only one service in the world, it would be *The Elliott Wave Financial Forecast*, written monthly by Steve Hochberg and Pete Kendall. It is just indispensable. We have a package offer, too, called the Financial Forecast Service (FFS), which includes the *Financial Forecast*, our Short Term Update, posted three times a week, and my monthly *Elliott Wave Theorist*. We have a European and Asian version of these services as well. Given unlimited funds, I would add all ten of the services listed above.

Useful Newsletters in a Bear Market

At all times ideally, but particularly in a global bear market, you need input from seasoned analysts who cover the financial world with healthy skepticism and are as good at warning you about what investments to avoid as they are at suggesting what actions to take. Here are a few that I like:

The Casey Daily Dispatch (free blog/email)
Interviewee: Doug Casey
Website: www.caseyresearch.com

The Gloom, Boom & Doom Report
Editor: Marc Faber
Website: www.gloomboomdoom.com
Email: info@gloomboomdoom.com

Address: Suite 801, The Workstation
43 Lyndhurst Terrace, Central
Hong Kong
Phone: (U.S. dial 011) 852-2-801-5410
Fax: 852-2-845-9192

Grant's Interest Rate Observer
Editor: James Grant
Address: 20 Wall Street, Suite 603, New York, NY 10005
Phone: 212-809-7994
Fax: 212-809-8492
Website: www.grantspub.com
Email: subscriptions@grantspub.com

SafeWealth Report
Production Manager: Jane V. Scott
Email: clientservices@safewealthadvisory.com
Address: SafeWealth Advisory Ltd. – Service Center,
P.O. Box 1995, Windsor, Berkshire SL4 5LL, U.K.
Phone: (in U.S., dial 011) 44-1753-554-461
Fax: (in U.S., dial 011) 44-1753-554-642

All that most of these services can do is offer you ideas. In the end, you will have to make up your own mind with the evidence that they present.

Chapter 22:

How To Ensure Your Physical Safety

This book focuses mostly on finance. If you get out of investments that will lose most of their value in a crash and keep your money safe, you will be quite wealthy in terms of your purchasing power. Unfortunately, that's not all there is to a major bear market. Depressions are a mess. You may have money, but certain goods might be scarce or rationed. You might be financially smart yet get caught in a war zone.

It may not be much fun to contemplate the social effects of downtrends, but it's important. If you remain financially sound, you will be positioned to take advantage of great investment opportunities, but if you encounter physical risk, you may not be around to do it.

Polarization and Conflict

The main social influence of negative social mood is to cause society to polarize in countless ways. That polarity shows up in every imaginable context — social, religious, political, racial, corporate and by class. The change is a product of the anger that accompanies negative mood, because each social unit seems invariably to find reasons to be angry with and to attack its opposing unit. During the 1930s-1940s bear markets, communists and fascists challenged political institutions. During the 1970s bear market, students challenged police, and blacks challenged whites. In both cases, labor challenged management and third parties challenged the status quo. When social mood is negative, rallies, marches and protests become common events. Separatism becomes a force as territories polarize. Populism becomes widespread as races and classes polarize. Third parties, fourth parties, and more, find constituents. Labor strikes, racial conflict, religious persecution, political unrest, trade protectionism, domestic repression, coups and wars become more common. One reason that conflicts gain such scope in depressions is that much of the middle class gets wiped out by the financial debacle, increasing the number of people with little or nothing to lose and anger to spare. To gain a good grounding in these dynamics, read *Socionomic Studies of Society and Culture* (2017).

The Chronically Erroneous Timing of Survival Concerns

In the 1950s, people built bomb shelters to guard against the risk of wars that had already ended. In the late 1970s and early 1980s, survival was a big topic. There were million-seller books about where to buy electric generators, how to choose bulletproof vests, storing dried foods and so on. This occupation coincided with an approaching major bottom of a 16-year bear market in the Dow/PPI. By then, you shouldn't have been wasting your time with it; you should have been buying stocks and bonds and making business plans. The ideal time to address safety concerns is at the beginning of a downtrend, not at the end.

Some Thoughts on Preparedness

Exactly what to do about your physical safety is a difficult problem. Living in a populous area or near a military installation or an important infrastructure site is dangerous in times of war or terrorism. If you are physically tied to a job in such a spot, decisions about relocating are even more difficult than otherwise.

I know people who have farmland in the country, a retreat in the mountains or a self-sufficient home. Others buy guns or learn self-defense. These are fine ideas if you can fit them into the requirements and desires of your life. But for such preparations to be useful, you have to find yourself in a position where you need them. Usually in a major bear market, you are less likely to encounter a mob, a criminal or a terrorist than to face state-sponsored controls within your own country or a military attack from without, in which cases there may be little that a retreat, a gun or karate lessons can do for you.

Nevertheless, if you determine that you need this type of preparation, now is a good time to dig out that old list of "Y2K" items and buy from it whatever you would like to have — such as an electric generator, a few months' worth of emergency dried foods, a video surveillance system, defensive weapons, etc. Being prepared for hard times is a comfort.

Here are some web locations to help you with aspects of physical preparedness. Some of them link to other sites, so once you get in the loop, you will find many more resources.

Disaster Preparedness

http://www.oism.org/nwss/s73p908.htm
http://www.fema.gov

Basic Survival

http://www.survivalcenter.com
http://www.ki4u.com/nuclearsurvival/list.htm

Home Security, Disaster Information

www.joelskousen.com

Dried Foods

www.alpineaire.com
spock.fcs.uga.edu/ext/pubs/html/FDNS-E-34-2.html
https://www.nal.usda.gov/fsrio

Self Defense

http://kravmagafederation.com/

Some disaster-related literature can be more upsetting than helpful. Always stop and think: Is this course of action necessary?

Is there a more sensible alternative? There is little point in taking much time, effort and cost to prepare for disastrous events that are highly unlikely or which can be judiciously avoided.

Preparation Pays

The coming crisis will be the most important influence on your personal and professional life for the duration. It will affect most things that happen to you, that you decide to do, or that you are forced to do. It will affect your business, your personal relationships, your friends and members of your family. You are part of society, so you are going to have to deal with the coming changes one way or another. The question is, will you deal with them from a position of strength and confidence, or will you react in panic along with everybody else? It is important to come to grips with the implications early. If you get your house in order before the new trend begins, you will be able to avoid much of the damage and, in fact, take advantage of the upcoming historic opportunities by calmly making opportunistic decisions when the time comes.

Preparing for a Change in Politics

Polarization in the political realm means radical politics. That much I can guarantee in the upcoming depression. Who wins the political battles is not scripted beforehand, except that incumbents tend to lose.

In the U.S. stock market collapse of 1835-1842, a brand-new political party (the Whigs) won the presidential election in 1840, and another (the Democrat Republicans), which had held power for forty years, soon afterward dissolved. In the election of 1860, following the stock market bottom and deep recession of 1857-1859, politics were so polarized that many states did not list all the presidential candidates on their ballots. A new party (Republican) won its first election. The following year, the Civil War broke out. The election of 1932, which took place near the bottom of the Great Depression, was less tense but still a watershed, as it accelerated the transformation of the United States into a semi-socialist state.

Given the projected size of the coming bear market, look for nations and states to split and shrink. Look for regional governments to challenge national ones. There is no way to know exactly where such splits will erupt, but erupt they will.

International politics will become increasingly dangerous. The number of annual nuclear weapons detonations, whether for testing purposes or attack, waxes and wanes inversely with the stock market. (For a graph, see Figure 1 in Chapter 16 of *The Socionomic Theory of Finance*.) Look for an increased number of nuclear explosions during the bear market. If you think weapons might be aimed at a spot near where you live, consider moving.

Debt and fiat money create political risks. Overseas investors and central banks own 42.5% of the U.S. Treasury's bonds in the marketplace. The largest investors are Japan and China. Ultimately, the turmoil of a record-breaking debt liquidation could force some governments to renege on some of their obligations, which could have extreme political consequences. On the other hand, an irony arises in the area of currency. The Fed's September 2016 bulletin reported that an estimated 75% of the new $100 bills ordered by the Federal Reserve Bank of New York are used to "satisfy foreign demand." Since 75% of dollar currency now resides overseas, a major dollar-based credit deflation would transfer 75% of the surviving dollars' expanding purchasing power to non-U.S. holders of dollar bills. Americans hold a larger percentage of IOUs, while others hold a larger percentage of the real thing, that is, to the extent that today's money is real. As noted in Chapter 19, President Roosevelt confiscated Americans' gold in 1933 and handed them a bag full of paper dollars in exchange. This time, one or more governments might decide to confiscate local or foreign cash currency in exchange for an electronic entry, to shore up the local banking system or to fight the drug war or terrorism. It might be prudent therefore to hold currencies of multiple, historically stable countries, such as

U.S. dollars, Canadian dollars and Swiss francs. What other political decisions such a situation may cause are anyone's guess, and so are the consequences. To get a handle on the ways in which social mood determines the political climate, see *Socionomic Causality in Politics* (2017).

What To Do If You Have Political Aspirations

If you have political aspirations and a major bear market occurs, you want to run for office near the bottom. You will be revered by the public and historians if you win. George Washington, Abraham Lincoln, Franklin Roosevelt and Ronald Reagan were all elected at or near major reversals in the stock market from down to up, and all have an exalted place in American history.

Third parties do well in tough times; so do outsiders and radicals; incumbents do poorly. If you want to be a politician, plan to run for office on any party ticket but that of the leader(s) in your country who rode the trend down.

Why Politics Matter in the Context of This Book

At some point during a financial crisis, money flows typically become a political issue. You should keep a sharp eye on political trends in your home country. In severe economic times, governments have been known to ban foreign investment, demand capital repatriation, outlaw money transfers abroad, close banks, freeze bank accounts, restrict or seize private pensions, raise taxes, fix prices and impose currency-exchange values. They have used force to change the course of who gets hurt and who is spared, which invariably means that the prudent are punished and the thriftless or the powerful are rewarded, reversing the result from what it would be according to who *deserves* to be spared or hurt. In extreme cases, such as when authoritarians assume power, they simply appropriate or take *de facto* control of your property.

You cannot anticipate every possible law, regulation or political event that will be implemented to thwart your attempt at safety, liquidity and solvency. This is why you must plan ahead and pay attention. As you do, think about these issues so that when political forces troll for victims, you are legally outside the scope of the dragnet.

How To Identify a Safe Haven

The real risk of social unrest will probably involve not so much roving itinerant bands looting your home — a classic fear that is rarely realized — as much as *international conflict* and *domestic repression*. In a bear market, both international and domestic tensions increase, and the resulting social actions can be devastating.

Far more people in the past century had their lives wrecked or terminated by domestic repression than by war. Whether you lived in Russia in the 1920s, Germany in the 1930s, Europe, China or North Korea in the 1940s, Cuba in the late 1950s, Cambodia in the 1970s or Venezuela in recent years, the smart thing to do early was to get out of Dodge. If you ever make such a decision, however, you will have to be lucky as well as smart. The people in Europe who decided in 1937 to move away before things got worse were the prudent ones. But one or two of them might have said, "Let's go somewhere far away and safe. Let's live on one of those sleepy islands in the Philippines." In other words, you might guess wrong.

One good guide to the world's developing crisis spots is Richard Maybury's *Early Warning Report*. If you are a European, Asian, African or Middle Eastern resident, his analysis is especially pertinent. Maybury has also published some excellent primers on inflation and justice. You may contact him through the following means:

Early Warning Report
Editor: Richard Maybury
Address: P.O. Box 84908, Phoenix, AZ 85701
Phone: 800-509-5400 and 602-252-4477
Fax: 602-943-2363
Website: www.richardmaybury.com
Email: pmc701@aol.com

If you live in a country with unstable politics, you should think about where you might go if things get oppressive. As with every aspect of a developing crisis, it is imperative to be prepared well before you have to make a final decision.

Some readers, admittedly only a few, may find merit in the idea of spending some time outside of their home countries as a depression unfolds. After researching the international scene for free and stable, Western-style, English-speaking countries, I find five top candidates: the United States, Canada, Australia, New Zealand and Ireland.

For specific information about these countries' visitation and extended visitation policies, investigate the following websites:

United States: www.travel.state.gov/content/travel.html
Canada: www.cic.gc.ca/english
Australia: www.immi.gov.au
New Zealand: www.immigration.govt.nz
Ireland: www.justice.ie

Some of these sites are easier to use than others; you may have to poke around to find what you want. Sometimes web addresses change. If any of these sites move, or if you wish to investigate countries other than those listed above, just perform an Internet search on key words. Most immigration offices have their own websites.

The world's #1 choice for refuge has long been the United States. Indeed, the philosophical foundation of the United States and its embodiment by many of its citizens may bode well for a low likelihood of severe domestic repression. Nothing is impossible, of course, and the history of civilizations suggests that, on a multi-century basis at least, the peak of U.S. world power is at hand and repression will follow. Potentially more dangerous is the international threat. The U.S.'s penchant for involving itself in other countries' disputes and provoking annoyance has made it a prime target for terrorists and certain governments. Any sustained or coordinated effort by America's enemies could make domestic life frightening and highly unstable. Alternatively, if authoritarians assume power at the federal level near the bottom of a depression (which happened throughout Europe and Asia in the 1930s and 1940s), difficulties could arise from domestic sources.

Simply *preparing* to move might not prove to be enough. Before you actually take that crucial action, your country of choice might shut its borders. Your country of *origin* might shut its borders. If terrorists infect a city in your nation with a biological warfare agent, you may be banned from entering any other nation. If you ever reach the point that you are sure you want a foreign refuge, you should move right then. If you choose a safe haven, and if the threats pass, you can always return to your home country.

At minimum, make sure that your passport is current, since demand for passports may increase later, delaying processing. Another great idea is to obtain a permanent resident visa in the country to which you would probably move if you came to such a decision. Like everything else, though, getting an extended visa takes time. You have to fill out forms, pay fees, and meet fairly stringent requirements. Even if you are quick and efficient, your legal representative or your host government might not be. Silly roadblocks can crop up that require another piece of paper, and so on. Some countries prohibit longterm visas for people beyond a certain age. The point is, to get what you want, act early. Before actually packing up to move, you should consult an attorney in your chosen country so that you can expedite the process.

I thought about filling up a couple of chapters with the pros and cons of these and other nations, but in the end, what really matters is what matters to *you*. Some of these countries have a better set of laws, others better weather, others a better culture, others better infrastructure, others more convenience. I am unfamiliar with non-English speaking countries that other people have been recommending, such as Argentina, Chile and Costa Rica, partly for the reason that I am unconvinced that they would be stellar havens of peace in a global depression. There are also many beautiful small island countries around the world, which rarely seem to be the focus of international conflict. You will have to sift through the websites, books and brochures and decide for yourself. Of course, the best way to approach such a question is to visit selected locations personally. They make great vacation spots, so you will hardly regret it. Who says contemplating a depression can't have its pleasures?

Chapter 23:

Getting Your Personal Financial Affairs in Order

Calling in Loans and Paying off Debt

People and institutions that best weather the system-wide debt liquidation of a deflationary crash and depression are those that take on *no debt* and extend *no risky credit*. This is the ideal situation for most people most of the time, anyway.

In this book, we have already covered many topics that pertain to the problem of risky credit. Make sure that you do not lend your money to weak borrowers, whether they be individuals, corporations or governments. If you have already done so, trade it for something better.

There is also the question of personal loans. Have you lent money to friends, relatives or co-workers? The odds of collecting any of these debts are usually slim to none, but if you can prod your personal debtors into paying you back before they get further strapped for cash, it will not only help you but it will also give you some additional wherewithal to help those very same people if they become destitute later.

If at all possible, remain or become debt-free. Being debt-free means that you are freer, period. You don't have to sweat credit card payments. You don't have to sweat auto repossession, ejection from your home or the loss of your business. You don't have to work 6% more, or 10% more, or 20% more just to stay even.

If you can afford it, the best mortgage is none at all. If you own your home outright and you lose your job, you will still have a residence. When banks are throwing others out of their homes, you will still have a place to live. If you can't pay the rent on your business space, you can move your business into your house. And so on. I would rather own a crackerbox dwelling outright than have a mansion with mortgage payments I can barely make.

Consider the bank's situation in times of financial stress. Suppose you have paid off enough of your mortgage so that you own 32% of your home, which reflects the average equity held by mortgage holders nationwide. Suddenly, you find that you can't make further payments because of money problems in a depression. At that point, even if house prices had fallen by over half, your bank would see it as no drop at all. It can place your property (actually *its* property) on the market. If the house sells for only 40% of its peak value, the bank gets 100% of its outstanding loan back. You can see why banks are pressured to sell properties in such situations. Of course, you end up homeless after slaving to pay off half the mortgage on the house over many years. That's what happens to many homeowners in a depression.

One way out of a debt load is personal bankruptcy. I don't recommend it, because it isn't honest. People lent you their hard-earned money; you should pay it back. If you truly are a victim of unforeseen circumstances and must declare bankruptcy, apologize to your creditors and tell them that you hope the experience taught them a lesson about under-collateralized lending.

What You Should Do If You Run a Business

Avoid long-term contracts with employees and contractors. Try to locate in a state with "at-will" employment laws. Red tape and legal impediments to firing could bankrupt your company in a financial crunch, thus putting everyone in your company out of work.

If you run a business that normally carries a large inventory (such as an auto or boat dealership), try to reduce it. If your business requires certain manufactured specialty items that may be hard to obtain in a depression, stock up.

If you are an employer, start making plans for what you will do if the company's cash flow declines and you have to cut expenditures. Would it be best to fire certain people? Would it be better to adjust all salaries downward an equal percentage so that you can keep everyone employed?

A cynic might recommend that if you are an employer, you should try to pay employees in stock or options, but if you share the expectations presented in this book, that course of action would be dishonest. Besides, an employee who gets gypped is hardly going to serve your company well. Don't forget, depressions don't last forever; when the next upturn comes, you will want a loyal staff to help you prosper in it, and they will want a healthy company to help them prosper, too. To encourage that result, pay what and how you need to for the talent you require.

If you manage a bank, insurance company, money management firm or other financial institution, work your way out of speculative derivative positions, especially bullish ones. Reduce stock market risk as much as possible. If you must be heavily invested in stocks — for example if you manage a stock mutual fund — hedge your positions with options. Tidy up your mortgage portfolio. Get rid of all second-tier debt paper. If you have invested in municipal bonds, consumer debt, real estate debt, junk bonds or anything other than top-grade paper, sell it at today's lofty prices. Get on a solid footing with investments that are high quality, liquid and commonly understood.

Perhaps most important, plan how you will take advantage of the next major bottom in the economy. Positioning your company properly at that time could ensure success for decades to come.

What You Should Do if You Are an Employee

If you have no special reason to believe that the company you work for will prosper so much in a contracting economy that its stock will rise in a bear market, then cash out any stock or stock options that your company has issued to you (or that you bought on your own).

If your remuneration is tied to the same company's fortunes in the form of stock or stock options, try to convert it to a liquid income stream. Make sure you get paid actual money for your effort.

If you have a choice of employment, try to think about which job will best weather the coming financial and economic storm. Then go get it.

If you are entrepreneurial, start thinking of ways to serve people in a depression so that you will prosper in it. Think about what people will need when times get hard. Some people automatically think that providing services for strapped people is the right choice when they think "depression." Certainly, opportunities are there. At the same time, that's not where most of the money is. Many people will *not* have their assets tied up in the stock market or other risky investments, and if deflation occurs, their real purchasing power will soar. At the bottom of the Great Depression, 75% of employable people had jobs, and they were quite well off. You can prosper by providing services to the solvent and the wealthy. Offering services to creditors may also yield steady employment. For example, because so much of today's debt is consumer debt, the repo business will probably thrive. There will also be a boom in bankruptcy services in a depression; maybe you can keep out of debt by helping others manage theirs.

If you have charitable impulses, this is the time to exercise them. Government services will shrink in a depression, and many people will be suffering. If you are *really* creative, find a way to help destitute people and make money doing so.

I don't have all the answers for your situation. You know your skills and tastes better than I do. Now is the time to take account of them.

Chapter 24:

Should You Rely on Government To Protect You?

In one sense, the answer is yes. You always have to live somewhere. If you are fortunate enough to live in a safe, free country, you can probably tell that those benefits are greatly a product of its philosophy of government. To that extent, you should rely on the best government you can find. Other than that, government can be a disappointing guardian.

Compounding the Problems

Government is rarely prepared for national financial calamities or economic depressions, and when it is, such events are unlikely to occur. This is a result of collective human nature. People are often prepared for the immediate past but rarely for the future.

Generally speaking, the intelligent way for an individual to approach the vagaries of his or her financial future is to have savings or buy insurance. Governments almost invariably do the opposite. They spend and borrow throughout the good times and find themselves strapped in bad times, when tax receipts fall. They have no savings, no nest egg, no emergency funds at all when they need them, just a mass of debt, crippling interest payments and declining income. Like their counterparts around the world, the Social Security, Medicare, Medicaid, SNAP (formerly "food stamps") and other wealth-transfer systems in the U.S. have been dispersing billions of dollars throughout decades of mostly good times.

When the bust occurs, governments won't have the money required to service truly needy people in unfortunate circumstances. They are likely then to make things worse by extending "unemployment benefits," which sucks money away from employers and makes them lay off more workers, by raising the cap on Social Security taxes, which takes money away from employers and employees and makes them less able to save and spend, and by increasing taxes generally, which impoverishes productive people so that they cannot invest. It's sad, but the pattern is almost always the same.

Dependencies To Avoid

Don't rely on government programs for your old age. Retirement programs such as Social Security in the U.S. are wealth-transfer schemes, not funded insurance, so they rely upon the government's tax receipts. Likewise, Medicaid is a federally subsidized, state-funded health insurance program, and as such, it relies upon transfers of states' tax receipts. When people's earnings collapse in a depression, so will the amount of taxes paid, which will force the value of wealth transfers downward. Every conceivable method of shoring up these programs can lead only to worse problems. A crisis in government wealth-transfer programs is inevitable.

Don't rely on projected government budgets. In 1835, after over two decades of economic boom, U.S. government debt became essentially fully paid off for the first (and only) time. In 1999, the federal deficit fell to zero. Conventional economists cited such conditions as bullish "fundamentals." (Any time an analyst claims to be using "fundamentals" for macroeconomic or financial forecasting, run, don't walk, to the nearest exit.) In actuality, those degrees of government solvency occurred the very years of major highs in the stock market that preceded protracted bear markets and severe economic contractions. Government surpluses generated by something other than a permanent policy of thrift are the product of exceptionally high tax receipts during boom times and therefore signal major tops. They're not bullish; they're bearish and ironically portend huge deficits directly around the corner.

Don't rely on any government's bank-deposit "insurance." The whole idea of having other banks and taxpayers guarantee bank deposits is theft in the first place and thus morally wrong and thus ultimately practically wrong. Government sponsored deposit insurance has lulled depositors into a false sense of security. After the 1930s, when thousands of banks failed, depositors became properly wary of profligate banks. Today they don't know or care what their bank officers are doing with their money, because they think the government insures their deposits. Deposit insurance will probably save accounts in the first few distressed banks, but if there is a system-wide credit implosion, the FDIC will be unable to protect you.

Don't rely incautiously on government's obligations to you if you are a retired government worker. In Argentina in 2002, the government suspended state pension payments to 1.4 million retired state employees. It had no money to pay because times got tough, and, naturally, it had never saved when times were good. The same thing could happen to many governments around the world, whether national, state or local, which pay billions of dollars annually in pensions. All of them are dependent either upon wealth transfer or upon managed funds that may or may not be properly invested.

Don't rely on all governments to pay their debts. In the 1930s, Fulton County, Georgia, where I grew up, was formed from two bankrupt counties that defaulted on their bonds. By 1938, state and local municipalities had defaulted on approximately 30% of the total value of their outstanding debt. Much of it was eventually resolved; some wasn't. U.S. investors today own billions of dollars worth of municipal bonds, thinking they are getting a great deal because that bond income is tax-exempt. This tax break may be a bonus in good times, but like so many seemingly great deals, this one will ultimately trap investors into risky positions. Governments that have borrowed to the hilt are running deficits even in the recent boom, so the risk of default in a depression is huge. If the issuers of your tax-exempt bonds default, you will have the ultimate tax haven: being broke. Quite a few munis are "insured," which salesmen will tell you means the same as "guaranteed." Such guarantees work fine until defaults drag down the insurers. That is to say, when you really need the supposed guarantees, they can fail. Given the huge extent of today's municipal indebtedness, such failures are inevitable.

Don't rely on your central bank, either. Ultimately, it is not in control of your country's stock market, bond market, interest rates or economy. It mostly *reacts* to markets. People think that the Fed lowered interest rates in 2007-8. But the *market* lowered interest rates, and the Fed simply followed. Declining interest rates are not a "first cause" designed to induce borrowing; rather, a dearth of borrowing is a prior cause that makes interest rates decline. Interest rates on perceived safe debt always fall when an economy begins to deflate and contract. The record-breaking decline in short-term U.S.-government interest rates in 2007-2009 was not any kind of medicine but a symptom of illness. It was not primarily administered but an effect. Japan's prime interest rate likewise fell to nearly zero in the 1990s because of deflation. The big drop in the cost of borrowing didn't change the course of the economy in either case. Why? Because the economy was in charge of the drop. The most that a central bank can do is to distort normal market trends and make credit a bit tighter or looser than it would otherwise be. Unfortunately, every such distortion has a counterbalancing, market-induced correction later.

Don't rely on government to bail out the banking system. How many more bailouts can governments afford? If many big banks get in trouble, prudence will dictate that even the richest governments stand aside. If instead they leap unwisely into bailout schemes, they will risk damaging the integrity of their own debt, triggering a fall in its price. Either way, again, deflation will put the brakes on their actions.

Don't expect government services to remain at their current levels. The ocean of money required to run the union-bloated, administration-stultified public school systems will be unavailable in a depression. School districts will have to adopt cost-cutting measures. Encourage independent, entrepreneurial, low-cost, free-market solutions, which will benefit both children and teachers. The tax receipts that pay for roads, police and jails, fire departments, trash pickup, emergency (911) monitoring, water systems and so on will fall to low levels, and some of these services will be curtailed. Look for ways to get better services elsewhere wherever it is legal and possible.

Don't rely on government "watchdogs." They rarely foresee disasters. U.S. regulators did not anticipate the financial collapse of 2007-2009, and they won't foresee the next one.

Be smart. Don't let your financial future end up depending upon proceedings covered by C-Span.

Chapter 25:

A Short List of Imperative "Do's" and Crucial "Don'ts"

Recall the old Chinese glyph that entwines crisis and opportunity. Position yourself to take advantage of what's coming.

Don't:

- Generally speaking, don't own stocks.
- Avoid high-yield bonds like the plague.
- Don't own any but the most pristine bonds.
- Generally speaking, don't invest in real estate.
- Generally speaking, don't buy commodities.
- Don't invest in collectibles.
- Don't trust standard rating services.
- Don't presume that government agencies and central banks will protect your finances.
- Don't buy investments too soon just because they look cheap. They will probably get cheaper.

Do:

- Fight the inertia that will keep you from taking action to prepare for the downturn. Start taking steps now.
- Involve your significant others in your decisions. Put your home or business partners in tune with your thinking before it's too late.
- Talk to heavily invested parents or in-laws who may be planning to pass on their investments to you. See if you can get them to become safe and liquid.
- Think globally, not just domestically.
- Open accounts at two or three of the safest banks in the world.
- Invest in short-term money market instruments issued by the soundest governments.
- Own some physical gold and silver coins.
- Have some cash on hand.
- Make sure that you have insurance policies only with the safest firms, and make sure that they deal only with safe banks.
- If you are so inclined, speculate conservatively in anticipation of a declining stock market.
- If it is right for your circumstances, sell your business.
- Make a list of things you want to buy at much lower prices when they go on "liquidation sale."
- If you want to have kids, hurry up. Statistics show that fewer people feel like doing so during a bear market.

- Give friends a copy of this book.

- Contact the services mentioned in this book. I am a market analyst and forecaster, not a banker, insurer, money manager, institution rater, business strategist or investment advisor. These services can help guide you through the maze. Some of them can help you design your whole strategy in a matter of days.

- Plan how to take advantage of the next major uptrend. For example, go back to school during the decline and come out with extra skills just as the economy begins to recover. Apprentice in a job for low pay and learn enough to start your own business at the bottom so you can ride the next big upwave of prosperity. Investigate troubled businesses to buy at the bottom at deep discounts.

- Smile! because you will not be jumping out of the window; you'll be preparing for incredible opportunities.

What To Do at the Bottom of a Deflationary Crash and Depression

At the bottom of a crash and depression, reverse most of our investment "do's" and "don'ts." When Elliott waves, valuations and market sentiment indicate that the collapse is ending, take a good portion of your safely stored cash and do the following:

- Cover shorts and buy stocks of surviving companies at fire sale prices.

- Buy depressed bonds from issuers that have survived.

- Buy more gold, silver and gold-backed cryptocurrency.

- Buy new cryptocurrencies with innovative technologies.

- Buy prime pieces of investment property from distressed banks.
- Buy your favorite uninhabited home or mansion at pennies on the dollar.
- Buy the under-rented office building or the abandoned business facility you need, for the cost of back taxes.
- Buy your favorite art and collectibles at bargain prices.
- Buy your own business back, start a business, or buy a distressed business cheap.
- Choose your location well and remain watchful of world affairs, because wars often break out during or shortly after depressions. For more specifics, see The Socionomic Causality in Politics (2017).
- Sit back and watch the investment markets in which you have invested turn up strongly, surprising the world.

With crisis comes opportunity. In a few years, it will be time to buy financial assets and build businesses again. If you've implemented the strategies in this book, you'll be one of the few who can do so. You've survived! Now prosper!

Appendix: Services Designed to Help You Survive and Prosper in the Deflationary Depression

Suitability and Risk

Many of the services listed in this book are suitable for all investors. Some are suited only for those of a certain level of expertise, wealth and/or income. In pursuing your chain of inquiries, you may occasionally discover some financial services that are unavailable to certain investors who fail to meet legal and financial criteria required by their nations' Accredited, Qualified and/or Professional Investor rules. These rules may prohibit your access to services that authorities deem to be unsuitable for you. Entities that need to comply with such rules should be able to explain which rules, if any, pertain to you. As you explore and judge various courses of action, please forgive any entities that refuse to fulfill your desires because they are following legal requirements. I have endeavored to provide enough avenues of inquiry in this book so that readers at all strata of wealth — small to large — will find methods for protecting their capital in times of deflation and depression.

I have positive information and impressions about the service providers listed in this book and believe them to have integrity. Nevertheless, I cannot endorse or guarantee other people's products or services. Therefore, it is imperative that each reader do his own proper investigation regarding suitability. I have experience with many of these service providers or know their principals personally. You will probably get even better service if you mention that you read about them in this book.

Note: Contact information can change. If in doubt, check the web.

RECOMMENDED SERVICES

Consultants on the World's Safest Banks and Storage Facilities

SafeWealth Consultants Ltd.
Contact: Sr. Vice President Cari Lima
Email: clientservices@safewealthconsultants.com
Address: Service Center, Grand-Rue 114, 2nd Level East,
CH-1820 Montreux, Switzerland
Phone: (U.S. dial 011) 41-21-966-7200
Fax: (U.S. dial 011) 41-21-966-7201

SafeWealth Report: Complimentary upon request

Qualified institutions' typical minimums:
Banks: 1m. CHF
Gold acquisition and/or storage: $100,000
Silver, platinum, palladium: $200,000
Currency cash notes: 250,000 units
External asset managers: 3m. CHF

Managed Bear Funds

Comstock Capital Value Fund
Managers: Charles Minter and Dennis DeCore
Address: 24 S Main Street, Yardley PA 19067
Phone: 215-493-7076
Fax: 215-493-8083
Website: www.comstockfunds.com
Email: info@comstockfunds.com
Minimum: $1000 or $250 in an IRA

GAMCO Mathers Fund
Manager: Henry van der Eb
Address: One Corporate Center, Rye NY 10580

Phone: 800-422-3554
Website: www.gabelli.com
Email: info@gabelli.com
Minimum: $1000

Managers with a Safety or Bearish Orientation

GNS Hillier Capital
Director: Michael Smorch
Address: 250 Monroe Avenue, Suite 400
Grand Rapids, Michigan 49423
Phone: 616-886-3022
Email: michael@gnshillierpartners.com
Minimum: $2 million

Hussman Funds
Manager: John Hussman, PhD
Website: www.hussmanfunds.com
Phone: 800-487-7626; 513-326-3551
Minimum $1000/$500 for IRAs

Lang Asset Management, Inc.
President: Julie Kirkpatrick
Address: 5605 Glenridge Dr., Suite 1080
Atlanta, GA 30342
Phone: 800-732-4171 and 404-256-4100
Fax 404-256-1473
Website: www.langasset.com
Email: investments@langasset.com
Minimum: $200,000

Newsletters for Staying Globally Informed

The Casey Daily Dispatch (free blog/email)
Interviewee: Doug Casey
Website: www.caseyresearch.com

The Gloom, Boom & Doom Report
Editor: Marc Faber

Address: Suite 801, The Workstation,
43 Lyndhurst Terrace, Central, Hong Kong
Phone: (U.S. dial 011) 852-2-801-5410
Fax: 852-2-845-9192
Website: www.gloomboomdoom.com
Email: info@gloomboomdoom.com

Grant's Interest Rate Observer
Editor: James Grant
Address: 2 Wall Street, Suite 603,
New York, NY 10005
Phone: 212-809-7994
Fax: 212-809-8492
Website: www.grantspub.com
Email: subscriptions@grantspub.com

U.S. & World Early Warning Report
Editor: Richard Maybury
Address: P.O. Box 84908, Phoenix, AZ 85701
Phone: 800-509-5400 and 602-870-9329
Fax: 602-943-2363
Website: www.chaostan.com
Email: service@earlywarningreport.com

Physical Safety

This is a diverse field. See Chapter 22 for leads.

Real Money (Gold, Silver, Platinum) Account

GoldMoney
Director: Geoff Turk
Address: Net Transactions Limited, 1st Floor,
32 Commercial Street, St. Helier
Jersey, JE2 3RU, British Channel Islands
Phone: (U.S. & Canada) 855-583-4653
(UK & International) 44-1543-633-900
Fax: (U.S. dial 011) 44-1534-633-901
Website: www.goldmoney.com

Safety Ratings for U.S. Banks and Insurance Companies

for institutions only:

Egan-Jones Ratings Company
Website: www.egan-jones.com
President: Sean J. Egan

IDC Financial Publishing, Inc.
Website: www.idcfp.com
Email: info@idcfp.com
Address: P.O. Box 140, Hartland, WI 53029
Phone: 800-525-5457 and 262-367-7231
Fax: 262-367-6497

Veribanc, Inc.
Website: www.veribanc.com
Email: service@veribanc.com
Address: P.O. Box 608, Greenville, RI 02828
Phone: 800-837-4226
Fax: 401-531-2290

Weiss Ratings, LLC
Website: www.weissratings.com
Address: 15430 Endeavour Dr., Jupiter FL 33478
Phone: 877-934-7778
Fax: 561-277-2576

Treasury-Only Money Market Funds

American Century Capital Preservation Fund I
Phone: 800-345-2021
Website: www.americancentury.com

Dreyfus 100% U.S. Treasury Money Market Fund
hone: 800-782-6620
Website: www.dreyfus.com

Vanguard Federal Money Market Fund
Phone: 877-662-7447
Website: www.vanguard.com

U.S. Gold, Silver and Coin Dealers

American Federal Rare Coin & Bullion, Inc.
President: Nick Grovich
Address: PO Box 5810, Carefree, AZ 85377-5810
Phone: 800-221-7694 or 480-553-5282
Fax: 480-553-5290
Website: www.americanfederal.com
Email: info@americanfederal.com

FideliTrade, Inc.
President: Jonathan Potts
Address: 3601 North Market Street, Wilmington, DE 19802
Phone: 800-223-1080 and 302-762-6200
Fax: 302-762-2902
Website: www.fidelitrade.com
Email: info@fidelitrade.com

Hancock & Harwell
President: Robert L. Harwell
Address: Suite 310, 3155 Roswell Rd, Atlanta, GA 30305
Phone: 404-261-6565
Fax: 404-237-6500
Website: www.raregold.com
Email: info@ raregold.com

Investment Rarities, Inc.
President: James R. Cook
Address: 7850 Metro Parkway, Bloomington, MN 55425
Phone: 952-853-0700 or 800-328-1860
Website: www.investmentrarities.com
Email: contact@investmentrarities.com

Miles Franklin Ltd.
President: Andrew Schectman

Address: 801 Twelve Oaks Center Drive, Ste 834
Wayzata, MN 55391
Phone: 800-822-8080 and 952-929-7006
Fax: 952-476-7971
Website: www.milesfranklin.com
Email address: andy@milesfranklin.com

Straight Talk Assets, Inc.
President: Glenn R. Fried
Address: P.O. Box 1301, Gainesville, GA 30503
Phone: 800-944-9249 and 770-536-8045
Website: www.coinmoney.com
Email: straighttalk@mindspring.com

Watching the Fed

Federal Reserve Board
Phone: 202-452-3819
Website: www.federalreserve.gov

Ludwig von Mises Institute
Address: 518 West Magnolia Avenue,
Auburn, AL 36832
Phone: 334-321-2100
Fax: 334-321-2119
Website: www.mises.org
Email: contact@mises.org
Book catalog: www.mises.org/store/Books-C1.aspx

The Money Market Observer
Chief Economist: Lou Crandall
Wrightson ICAP, LLC
Address: Harborside Financial Center, Plaza V
Jersey City, NJ 07311
Phone: 212-815-6540
Fax: 212-341-9103
Website: www.wrightson.com
Email: sales@wrightson.com

Wave Analysis and Economic Forecasting

Elliott Wave International, Inc.
President: Robert R. Prechter
Address: P.O. Box 1618, Gainesville, GA 30503
Phone: 800-336-1618 and 770-536-0309
Fax: 770-536-2514
Website: www.elliottwave.com
Email: customercare@elliottwave.com
Paid services: Financial periodicals, global market coverage, opportunity alerts, intraday market analysis, books, online courses
Free services: Club EWI
Related websites:
www.socionomics.net
www.robertprechter.com

CPSIA information can be obtained
at www.ICGtesting.com
Printed in the USA
LVOW13*0334100418
572868LV00004B/5/P

9 781616 041007